MIRACLE out of the MUD

Living Proof that GOD Answers Prayer, and How He'll Answer Yours!

Limited Edition

Cleon Dewey

MIRACLE *Out of the* MUD

Limited Edition

ISBN: 978-1-929921-21-8 (Paperback)

Cover design: Daniel Larson, R & D Web Design

Interior design: Thomas Taylor

Published by:

VICTORY
PUBLISHERS
www.Victory-Publishers.com

MIRACLE

Out of the

MUD

Limited Edition

www.MiracleoutoftheMud.com

Once upon a time,
a seed was planted deep into the ground.
From the surface,
it was not apparent that anything was happening...
way down there in obscurity.
All the while it was changing
in the moist environment.
The seed was involved in a wondrous process.

Seasonal rains fell.
Storm winds blew relentlessly across the barren
land. Winter's blizzard came and went.
Alas, the long awaited sunshine returned.
But the surface of the earth
had become very hard and dry.
Hope was lost for the seed...
buried in darkness.
It was even forgotten.
Unbeknownst,
in the depths, was the mud from yesterday's rain.
The mud...yes, the mud had gently protected the
seed of promise.

On a future day,
a tiny hint of something green could be seen,
poking through the crusty topsoil.
Behold! One determined blade broke forth.
The forgotten seed had overcome!
It survived the terrible seasons
and it continued growing
until it became strong and viable.
Today, it stands tall and victorious, miraculously
bearing the precious fruit of its purpose.
That is the essence of a
"MIRACLE *Out of the* MUD."

Contents

www.MiracleoutoftheMud.com

Foreword

There's nothing that pleases a physician more than seeing a patient respond to medical treatment and regain vitality. Cleon Dewey is my patient and I have known her family for many years. When we met, she faced recurring colon cancer and was in grave condition.

When I read this book, I was struck with the realization that it is more than an account of her journey back to good health. It is a powerful, personal testimony. Not only is she cancer-free today, but she found the courage to write her compelling story and share her faith that was key in her recovery.

"MIRACLE *Out of the* MUD" is a fascinating, must-read for anyone facing the difficulties of life, chronic illness or who is in search of spiritual strength.

John E. Anderson, MD
The Frist Clinic
Nashville, Tennessee

Introduction

*D*o you need a miracle to pull you out of your "mud"?

When cancer descended suddenly on me, and the doctor said I had three months to live, I dug deep into the reservoir of my faith. What I found changed me. The Word of God took root and became sustenance to my spirit, soul and body. I was calmly assured that God was not surprised by my circumstance; indeed, He was right there...taking me through, from the darkness of a death sentence, into the light of joyful, purposeful life...all for His glory.

My friends said, "Someone may die needlessly if you don't share your story." This book may save your life, or the life of someone close to you. I pray you find answers to questions screaming in your heart, and a path to victory, in its pages. It should at least persuade you that God hears *and* answers prayer, and He'll answer yours...He may be answering yours right now.

Every person in this muddy world is going through *something*. Your mud may be different from mine and perhaps even more tragic than two terminal cancers. It's not the mud that matters...it's the Master. I stand confident that the grace of God, that brought me through my mud, will surely bring you through yours.

Everyone has a choice: curse the mud, or celebrate a miracle in the making!

I invite you to laugh and cry with me. Join me as we come face to face with the Master, who used mud to restore a blind man's sight long ago. Together, let's deal with our mud. Let's behold Him clearly, and give Him praise, honor and glory, for both the miracle *and* the mud.

My stomping grounds were the high plains of West Texas in the small towns of Lamesa and Littlefield. Truman and Pauline Cotton were loving parents to me and my older brother, Clois.

My wonderful husband, Levoy, and I met at Southwestern University, a small Bible School in Waxahachie, Texas. A singer and musician long before we met, Levoy was called to the ministry of evangelism with an emphasis on music. He was the director of music and youth for churches in Texas and Missouri for about the first six years of our marriage, while I played the piano.

Our daughters, Cindy and Susie, were four and five years old when we moved to Nashville, Tennessee, and started traveling full time. For the next 20 years we booked an average of 300 engagements annually. For the first five years, Levoy's brother, Tim, and his wife, Sheryl, were part of our original group, "The Singing Deweys." We recorded three albums with Hymntone Records in Mechanicsburg, PA, and the Heartwarming label of the Benson Company in Nashville. We also released five children's albums, featuring our little girls. Levoy, Cindy, Susie and I played keyboards, saxophone, clarinet, flute, bassoon, banjo, guitar, mandolin, upright bass and other instruments. We also made four instrumental albums. We have produced and participated in dozens of gospel records, tapes, and CD's. God inspired us to write many songs, including *"Heaven's Sounding Sweeter."* Our travels have taken us across the United States and to world mission outreaches in 33 foreign countries.

Cindy and Susie were schooled on a converted bus, rolling down the highways of America en route to concerts and services. One day I hope to pass along the fascinating adventures of our traveling experiences and the encounters that colored our lives.

Cindy married Mark Larson and they have three children: Rachel, Daniel and Andrew. Suzanne

(Susie) married Nathan Young and they have two boys, Elijah and Benjamin. Our two delightful daughters and their families are the joy of our lives. You will get to know them better as you read.

The message we have delivered has not changed, lo these many years, although the method has. The anointing upon the music and the Word still breaks the yoke of bondage. We are amazed by the providence of the Almighty and the circumstances He allows to make us better-conditioned vessels.

1

Prepare the Soil

*T*he bleeding and pain that had plagued my body for several months could no longer be ignored. Keeping secrets from Levoy was not my habit, but I felt I had to handle the problem myself. Something unusual was happening to me, but I did not wish to disrupt our lives. With our busy traveling schedule, we had precious little time to ourselves, and taking sick days was out of the question...so I thought. I have always seen the glass half full, so it was easy to put my concerns aside and deal with them at a more convenient time. Still, my sleep was interrupted by nagging suspicions about my health.

> *Could it be that Daddy's recent death has made me more sensitive about my own mortality? Maybe I have an overactive imagination and things are not as bad as they seem.*

I was not aware of it at first, but God was preparing the soil of my heart for a very different season.

*Lord, You have heard the desire of the humble;
You will prepare their heart...* (Psalm 10:17 – NKJV)

When my mother visited us in Nashville, I casually mentioned that I was passing blood. The crochet in her eighty-plus year old hands quickly dropped to her lap. She fixed her piercing green eyes on her only daughter, leaned slightly forward, and pressed for more details. I took a deep breath and tried to appear casual as I described the symptoms. I reassured her, "Don't worry about it, Mother. There's probably nothing to be concerned about."

What was I thinking? I've said too much already. Oh, if only I could retrieve those words that escaped my mouth. But it's too late, now.

Mother slept little that night.

I was usually the first one in the household to arise. When aroma of the freshly brewed coffee from the automatic pot wafted across my senses, I would be on my feet and ready to greet the day. On this particular morning I was surprised to see Mother sitting at the kitchen table waiting for me. She held a medical book from the house library. Her worries over what had been said the evening before prompted her to do some research. The somber countenance etched on her face indicated that she had discovered some unsettling facts. She was convinced that I had signs of colon cancer.

As I reached into the cupboard for two cups and poured the steaming coffee, her troubled gaze followed my every move. I attempted to change the subject...nothing doing. By nature, Mother was not pushy, but this time she could not be dissuaded. I leaned across the table, patted her hand, still clutching the medical book, and promised to call my doctor soon. Next week would be a better time. A doctor's appointment would put a damper on the special plans we had made for each day of her visit. The words sounded hollow as I reminded her that the offices at the hospital didn't open until 9:00 a.m. She watched the clock. At exactly five minutes after the hour she handed me the phone.

Dr. Benjamin Caldwell had been my gynecologist for more than twenty years. He knew I was not easily shaken. After his nurse explained the urgency, he worked me in his schedule the next day. What I heard in his office stunned me. After a thorough examination, Dr. Caldwell was certain that I had advanced colorectal cancer. I had never seen him appear that somber; the look on his face spoke volumes. His assistant immediately called a specialist, whose office was directly across the street. Dr. Caldwell told me later, "I thought I was looking at a walking dead woman."

Dr. Benjamin Fisher was one of the leading colorectal surgeons in the southeast. His voice sounded strangely far away when he pronounced his diagnosis: "You have colorectal cancer." It was Suzanne's birthday, September 5, 1994. It seemed inappropriate to hear such news on my daughter's special day.

Who is he talking to?

I glanced nervously around the room, but I could not escape the fact that he was talking to me. For an instant, my brain could not absorb what I was hearing.

The instinct to defend myself kicked into gear. Questions tumbled out of my dry mouth, one after another. "I am not that sick. Are you *sure* this is cancer? Don't you know that I've had these same symptoms *before,* and they weren't *serious*?" The argument indicated serious denial.

I was the only one talking. Levoy's hand was on my shoulder. Cindy bit her lip, holding back tears. The cold leather of the chair was bone-chilling. My mind was whirling. I felt vulnerable, too shocked to cry. I wanted to run.

Dr. Fisher explained the prognosis in layman's terms. "The cancer is a fast moving lesion that involves the rectal muscle. That complicates everything. Cancer is even more critical when a muscle is involved, because of the blood supply. This usually impedes the cure. Its very nature complicates the possibility of stopping the spread of disease. You have a big problem with this thing."

His plan of action was decisive. He stressed the urgency of starting treatments as soon as possible. Arrangements for chemotherapy and radiation would be set within the next two days. The objective was to reduce the tumor, which was the size of a tennis ball. Surgery was not feasible at that time. The cancer was aggressive and drastic measures had to be taken to shrink the mass and annihilate it, if possible. Nothing would be spared, medically speaking, to stop this rapidly moving killer.

Everything was happening too fast.

He must be talking about someone else...another patient. Yes, that's it. He has the wrong information. That's probably not even my folder in his hand. Dr. Caldwell said, just yesterday, that I have symptoms of cancer. But, Dr. Fisher...he's a specialist. I didn't expect this.

Only a few days prior to Dr. Fisher's diagnosis, I had read an article in a popular magazine by a doctor in Europe who was a proponent of unconventional methods of curing cancer. I told Dr. Fisher that I remembered something about apricot seeds proving successful in the early treatment of malignant tumors. The doctor abruptly interrupted. Slightly built and in his early 70s, Dr. Fisher stood as he pushed back his chair; he leaned over his large mahogany desk, pointing a finger at me to emphasize the importance of what he said. He did not mince words or try to soften the blow; he cleared his throat and looked me squarely in the eyes, slowly pronouncing a death sentence: "Lady, please listen to me. You will not be here for Christmas if there's not a turnaround in your condition. There are no options. Once again, it's very late for you."

I sat motionless and listened to words I could not begin to comprehend. My trembling fingers counted on the surface of my purse.

October...November...December.

Three months to live. The words shocked me like a bolt of lightning. The prognosis could not be clearer. Dr. Fisher finally had my attention.

Oh, how I would like to say that I was totally engulfed by feelings of euphoric victory at that moment; that no prognosis could have a negative effect on me, but the truth was very different.

Many years ago, my father-in-law was knocked off a ladder by 440 volts of electricity and landed on his feet. Outwardly, Dad Dewey appeared to be fine, but he bore the inner effects of that trauma for the duration of his life. Hearing that I had terminal cancer, I looked okay from the outside, but inside I was emotionally ripped apart.

As Cindy, Levoy and I left the doctor's office, my eyes lingered for a moment on other patients. One scene captured my attention: a young woman was softly crying as she sat next to an older gentleman of Asian descent. "Probably his daughter," I thought. "I wonder what news they received."

You are probably not as bad as me. The doctor said I have three months. How much time do you have?

My world was suddenly upside down. Only yesterday the sky was perfectly clear. Something cruel, far beyond my control, had just robbed me of a future. I was still trying to wrap my brain around the horrific information that had bombarded me. One hour ago, there was so much to look forward to...now this.

The audacity! The pronouncement of my fate was spoken by someone I had just met. What right did that doctor have? My words were spent. There was no more energy for an argument. In my attempt to make the case that I was just fine, my emotional reserves were depleted. Somewhere deep within I knew the prognosis was established. Denial had to give way to reality.

Cindy dealt with the initial blow in her unique way. She believes the Bible, including the part that says a merry heart is like a medicine. The 20-minute drive home was probably not typical. My daughter instinctively reached for a new recording of a comedian, popped it in the machine, and cranked up the volume. That guy would make anybody laugh; even someone who had just been told she had three months to live! Cindy drove while we all laughed. A belly-laugh rolled out of me, like a rushing waterfall, and every other thought was drowned. It is proven that laughter produces endorphins that relieve stress and promote well being. Every one of those endorphins was put to good use that day.

When I got out of the car my legs felt weak. I could hardly stand. The ground seemed unsteady beneath me. Everything looked and felt surreal.

Surely, I would wake up and this nightmare would be over.

Mother, Suzanne, Nathan and little Rachel were waiting for us, holding a solemn vigil in the house. They made valiant attempts to be upbeat, but sadness, anguish, and unanswered questions were written on their faces. They were still reeling from the report they had heard on the telephone, only moments before we arrived. The atmosphere was charged with unfamiliar tension. For a brief moment, I wanted to bolt out the door. All eyes were fastened on me as I labored up the stairs.

If I could only get away from them, maybe it wouldn't hurt so much. I am the cause of all this trouble. If I hadn't gone to the doctor...things would be normal.

In spite of those fitful thoughts, an uncanny knowing dominated my senses. Mother's pressure on me to call the doctor had probably saved my life. Even so, I was conflicted. It was Rachel's first day of school. I was sorry that my health issues overshadowed this happy day for our first grandchild.

Would I be there to see her graduate...or go to the second grade?

The privilege of planning anything for the future was stripped away in one cruel moment. Life seemed so fragile...so unfair. "Three months" screamed in my head and made me hot with anger. Only yesterday, Levoy and I had exciting plans. We were booking services and making projections for the ministry. I had always considered myself a healthy woman. When I was sick, God healed me.

Would He heal me this time?

A killer cancer was stalking. This was very different from any other challenge Levoy and I had faced. I knew that the greatest test of my faith was upon me. I felt vulnerable, like an open target with no defense; one upon whom fate had turned its back. At the same time, I was confident that it would be okay. I knew that God could not fail.

More than anything, I wanted to be alone. I did not have a grip on the news I had received. I slipped into our bedroom and shut the door behind me. My emotions rode a roller coaster. I heard a scream. It was me! The pillow muffled the uncontrollable sobs and absorbed the tears. I could not block out the mocking of a strange hiss in my head.

"Three months...Three months...Three months."

I was exhausted. I cried out to God, "Why me... why this...why now?" I wept until there were no more tears. My throat ached from screaming. I listened to my own uneven breath and stared into nothingness.

> **I sink in deep mire, where there is no standing: I am come into deep waters, where the floods overflow me. I am weary of my crying: my throat is dried: mine eyes fail while I wait for my God.**
> (Psalm 69:2-3 - KJV)

Out of nowhere, a strong feeling of guilt smothered me. Raw emotions washed over me like waves of acid. Crazy thoughts invaded my mind like an army.

I must be a bad person, or this would not have happened. It is my fault! I have probably eaten the wrong foods or exposed myself unknowingly to toxic materials.

I felt stupid and ashamed, but I didn't understand why. After wallowing in a mire of self-pity and confusion, for what seemed like a very long time, I rebounded.

If I have only three months to live, I refuse to live them like this.

Sound thinking gradually returned. My resolve to get out of the pit of deprivation was powerful and I started moving. There was a Bible on my nightstand. It's not my style to randomly pick a verse, but this was not a time for the norm. I flipped open the Bible on the bed and watched as the pages settled. My eyes fell instantly upon a verse I had read before. Now I saw it much differently...with my heart.

Uphold me according unto thy word that I may live: and not be ashamed of my hope.
(Psalm 119:116 - KJV)

That was it! The Lord would heal me. He would protect me from evil. Yes, He would prepare me for what was to come. I would surely live and not die!

Of all the thousands of verses that might have caught my eye, that was the one that jumped off the page. My mind was renewed. My spirit was quickened and I knew that I knew. It would be okay. In an instant, the diagnosis came face to face with the truth of God's Word. It was the beginning of a miracle.

It was written in an old song, "Trouble is Thy servant that brings me to Thee." Down through the ages, God has used the troubles of life to draw mankind to Himself. It is human nature to seek the Lord more earnestly when trouble comes along. I began drawing upon the reservoir of my faith, knowing that no matter what transpired God would use it to His glory and my good. At the same time, I was curious to know what God would do this time...with cancer.

No one understands the necessity of preparation better than a farmer. My Granddad bought acreage in South Dakota in the early 1950's. The virgin land had never seen a plow. Preparing the grassy prairie for planting required a lot of hard work. Huge rocks that prevented tilling were dragged alongside the perimeter of the field, and the gaping holes left were tediously leveled. When the ground was finally ready, he pulled the big tractor onto the field. The aroma of fresh dirt, turning and yielding to the plow, quickened his senses. Precious seeds were sown into the ready soil. God sent the life-giving rain and welcome sunshine. In due season, Granddad gathered a bountiful harvest of golden grain. The fruit of his hard labor was at last a sweet reward.

Preparation creates a passage for the entrance of good things, but it is hard work and usually not a pretty part of the process. I was beginning to learn more about what it means to belong to the Master. When I received Christ as Savior, I gave him my heart. He has always known exactly what I need.

My obvious tragedy, cancer, was a tool in His skillful hands. He tenderly began the process of honing, shaping and molding me into a more pliable image. It hurt, and I did not understand. I was clay in the Master's hand and the tool He used was painful.

The things God often uses might be a broken relationship, a tragic accident, overwhelming disappointment or a chronic illness. The hurtful events of life are often instruments in the hands of a merciful God, which draw humanity unto Himself. Cancer was indeed a sharp, cutting instrument.

P R A Y E R

PREPARE!

The painful process of preparation enhances the ultimate purpose of one's existence.

The cause of pain in your life can be your greatest blessing if you surrender it to God in prayer. Think about Joseph in the book of Genesis. A string of unfortunate circumstances literally set him up to become the savior of his people.

> *...Joseph said to them, "Don't be afraid. Am I in the place of God? You intended to harm me, but God intended it for good to accomplish what is now being done, the saving of many lives."*
>
> (Genesis 50:20 & 21 - NIV)

Trouble is a tool that God has always used to prepare hearts. He may not create the bad things, but He gently and wisely uses them to accomplish His will. It's the conditioning of the heart that makes some people *better* in tough times, while others become *bitter*?

Your battle is winnable. Get ready, get armed, and get prepared to stand in triumph!

...put on the full armor of God, so that when the day of evil comes, you may be able to stand your ground, and after you have done everything, to stand...Stand firm... (Ephesians 6:13 & 14 - NIV)

PRAYER: *The winds of change are blowing. Without You, Lord, I would be so afraid. Your unconditional love is embracing me and preparing me to survive this storm in victory. Please use this season in my life to make me more like You.* AMEN.

2

Rise
Above the Storm

I could hardly wait to get out of the bedroom and tell everyone in the house what my heart knew: I had a promise from the Lord! Levoy and the family needed a positive report. Just enough grace to take that next step...that's all I had. All I could handle was one little baby step, and its discovery was pivotal in transforming my state of mind. The assurance from the Bible on my nightstand was enabling me to cope. God's Word was giving me courage to face the circumstances. The disease no longer loomed like an ominous threat. The promise was bigger than the problem.

A glance in the mirror prompted a quick touch-up. The distraught face looking back was that of a stranger. I grabbed a hairbrush, ran it through my rumpled hair and fumbled in the drawer for some lipstick. I found my drugstore eyelashes stuck to a pillow, and back they went on my swollen eyelids. Rachel was only six years old...too young to comprehend all this cancer stuff. It was time to see her "Mimi" with a happy face.

Isn't it amazing what a word from the Lord can do? I stepped out of the bedroom on wings of fresh hope, with head held high, clinging to *Psalm 119:116*. I shared that promise from the Psalmist David as a declaration of my trust in Him. My family stood with me, according to the scripture:

I tell you that if two of you on earth agree about anything you ask for, it will be done for you by my Father in heaven. (Matthew 18:19 - NIV)

We claimed the promise! Tears of joy flowed down our faces and praises ascended. We laughed and danced about the room in the face of the storm, because we believed the promise in His Word. For the rest of the afternoon, we reminded one another of other storms...other uncertain times when our backs had been against the wall. God had never failed. He was literally upholding me according to His Word, as in times past. Anticipation of God's intervention surged within my spirit.

I chided the girls, "Y'all can stay out of my stuff. Your Mama's not going anywhere." Cindy and Suzanne were never shy about going into my closet and borrowing anything they needed—well, almost anything. My girls and I have exchanged everything except shoes. All three of us are really glad we don't wear the same shoe size. My teasing comment was music to their ears. Everyone in the house knew I was back and in usual form.

Never shall I forget the next day, when I awakened on the brink of the greatest storm of my life. It was not one of those welcome thunder clouds that rained new life into the thirsty ground and made the skin tingle when the hot lightning bolts streaked across the big sky. I was living the real life experience of being caught in the midst of a killer storm that would seem overwhelming in days to come. The forecast was frightening and bleak. Fierce winds would blow against my vessel and would seem to be unbeatable.

Instant healing did not happen and I was disappointed. Although I had support of family and friends, I felt isolated. It was my personal storm and I had to go through it. No one could take my place. God's providence had allowed it to come and, by His grace, I would find the strength to rise above it.

I have experienced healing many times; sometimes instantly, and sometimes through a long process. The timing and outcome are God's business. Tongue in cheek, I used to say, "If you have a choice, take the quick one." I expected a miraculous healing that would astound the medical community. Then it came to me: God does not need my creative ideas to write my testimony. I knew that my prayers were not unanswered, only delayed.

Dr. Fisher pressed hard to schedule treatments. He put forth a precise plan of simultaneous chemotherapy and radiation. For the next week, precisely at 10:00 a.m., I received a call from his office. The message was always a solemn reminder that time was of the essence. Treatments must begin! I stalled. Making the choice to undergo chemotherapy and radiation was monumental.

God, I thought Psalm 119:116 was a promise that I would be healed! What am I to do?

Pressure to make a decision mounted, and so did the confusion. I thought submitting to medical solutions would negate divine healing, and I did not want to miss a great blessing by getting ahead of God's plan. Impatiently, I waited for signs that the situation was turning around. There were none. Meanwhile, my condition appeared to be declining. My body still had all the symptoms of cancer. The bleeding and pain were not going away.

Dark clouds were hanging low and the storm was encroaching upon the boundaries of my existence. It seemed that all the praying in the world would not change the inevitable. I knew the scripture:

> *...the effectual fervent prayers of the righteous avail much.* (James 5:16)

My human reasoning got in the way. I doubted. There were so many questions and so few answers.

Would I survive the fierce winds of this disease?

> *...When the enemy comes in like a flood, the spirit of the Lord will lift up a standard against him.*
>
> (Isaiah 59:19 - NKJV)

Isaiah was translated from Hebrew to Greek. A comma, which had initially been placed *before* the phrase, "*like a flood,*" was instead placed *after* the phrase. Changing the placement of that comma altered the verse. The present-day Greek translation, "*When the enemy comes in like a flood...*", emphasizes the negative forcefulness of the enemy. The original Hebrew version, in which the flood becomes a positive force, is powerful: "*...like a flood the Spirit of the Lord will lift up a standard against him.*"

If ever I needed the flood of the Spirit, it was the day that cancer slammed my world. I was cast down, but I was not destroyed.

We are troubled on every side, yet not distressed; we are perplexed, but not in despair; Persecuted, but not forsaken; cast down, but not destroyed; Always bearing about in the body of the dying of the Lord Jesus, that the life also of Jesus might be made manifest in our body. (II Corinthians 4:8-10 - KJV)

In 2005, during Hurricane Katrina, a renegade barge slammed into and breeched one of New Orleans' levees. The ominous, unseen danger was floating in the dark waters, but no one knew it was coming. Only God knows the renegade forces that threaten lives.

At first, a storm cell can hardly be seen with the naked eye. It might be a small abnormality, far away in the atmosphere. The small cell starts turning in a counter clockwise rotation and it continues to grow with every passing hour. The barometric pressure, water temperature, and other conditions determine the strength and size of a hurricane. These storms furtively maneuver through the atmosphere, gradually and steadily gathering momentum. The same is true with cancer. One little cell becomes two...two become four...four become eight. On it goes until it becomes catastrophic, like a hurricane. When the time is right, it unleashes a deadly fury.

As a hurricane approaches, forecasters can pinpoint its track and the exact location of landfall. The latest technology is utilized to warn the population of impending danger. There is usually a tiny window by which escape is possible. Those who heed the early warnings and evacuate, escape the brunt of attack. Others, not willing to comply, often pay with their property...and even their lives.

There are early warning signs of most diseases, including cancer. The percentages of those who observe early detection guidelines have a better outcome when disease is detected. Modern medicine has discovered many excellent measures of preventing some of the extreme ravages of cancer and even death. My victory over cancer proves that both medical intervention and faith in God work hand in hand.

What does one do when the Heavens are brass and God is silent?

I tried to read the Bible, but it was difficult to concentrate. I was clinging to a promise. The God I loved and served promised life, not sickening chemicals and burning sores from radiation. In the midst of that turbulence, something profoundly simple settled my spirit. According to His Word, He would not—He could not—forsake me, even though I was confused and disheartened. The knowledge of His Word was still embedded within my spirit, though my flesh was weak. It's amazing! The promise that I received, alone in my bedroom, continued ministering to me and calmed my anxiety. Still, my feelings vacillated wildly, because the sequence of events did not comply with my faith-plan. My soul remained anchored to the rock, even as the storm was raging.

The prayers of countless people ascended to the Father on my behalf. Only eternity will reveal the significance of prayer. I depended upon my family's spiritual insight and unwavering faith. They were united in wanting me to follow Dr. Fisher's plan. Still, surrendering to chemotherapy and radiation was appalling to me.

There is an old saying: "An idle brain is the devil's workshop." Fear of the chemicals and radiation was overwhelming. All of the horror stories I had ever heard about their side effects haunted me. Thankfully, fortification against the evil imagination of the enemy came by the daily renewing of my mind. Every page I read in God's Word encouraged me to seek higher ground...to run to Jesus. By His grace, I would rise above the fear.

And do not be conformed to this world, but be transformed by the renewing of your mind, that you may prove what is that good and acceptable and perfect will of God. (Romans 12:2 - NKJV)

One week, following the diagnosis of colorectal cancer, I was at home alone. My mind was consumed with one thing: what to tell the doctor. I started reading about Jesus' miracles in the Gospels. It became so clear: the growing cancer in my body was only part of the problem. Deadly chains of doubt and fear must be broken. The Bible says, **"the truth will set you free"** (John 8:32 - NIV).

The story of a blind man and the mud captured my imagination.

> *As he went along, he saw a man blind from birth. His disciples asked him, "Rabbi, who sinned, this man or his parents, that he was born blind?"*
>
> *"Neither this man nor his parents sinned," said Jesus, "but this happened so that the work of God might be displayed in his life. As long as it is day, we must do the work of him who sent me. Night is coming, when no one can work. While I am in the world, I am the light of the world."*
>
> *Having said this, he spit on the ground, made some mud with the saliva, and put it on the man's eyes. "Go," he told him, "wash in the Pool of Siloam" (this word means Sent). So the man went and washed, and came home seeing.*

His neighbors and those who had formerly seen him begging asked, "Isn't this the same man who used to sit and beg?" Some claimed that he was.

Others said, "No, he only looks like him."

But he himself insisted, "I am the man."

"How then were your eyes opened?" they demanded.

He replied, "The man they call Jesus made some mud and put it on my eyes. He told me to go to Siloam and wash. So I went and washed, and then I could see." (John 9:1-11) (NIV)

When Jesus and His disciples came upon the blind man, they inquired, *"Rabbi, who sinned, this man or his parents, that he was born blind?"* Those who walked the dusty roads with Jesus wanted to know the reason for the problem. Human nature wants to affix blame when things go wrong. We want immediate answers. The disciples were curious.

Notice Jesus' response to the question: *"...that the work of God might be displayed in his life."* The answer was simple and to the point. It is a proven fact that much sickness is a result of sinful living or irresponsible lifestyles. There is a price to pay for choices made. Seeds sown will bring a harvest, good or bad. That is no excuse to condemn other people. We should not judge another person or falsely accuse them. The reason and purpose for their mud is God's business.

The blind man literally came face to face with Jesus, and he was in worse condition than before. He was still blind, *and* dirty. Jesus told him to go to the pool in that condition. Some historians say it was about a two mile journey. He had to walk that great distance, all the while being harassed by the shrill voices of the naysayers.

Why would Jesus, who was God in the flesh, send a blind man on a journey that was so inconvenient? Getting to the pool was a huge challenge. He could have healed him then and there. Hadn't the blind man suffered long enough?

His neighbors, the Pharisees, ridiculed him and criticized Jesus for performing a miracle on the Sabbath. Even his parents were afraid to speak for fear of the Jews. The spirit of fear is not a new thing. The devil plays the same old tricks these days. His game is to spoil the works of righteousness. Anything that glorifies the Father is against the enemy of our souls.

The blind man was healed when he washed in the pool. Hallelujah! Forget the mud. Forget the cruel ridicule. Forget all of the inconvenience in making his way to the pool. Forget the embarrassment of his parents. *He could see!* Nothing else really mattered.

Jesus healed in *John 9* and Jesus heals today. The words of the healed man said it all: ***"One thing I do know. I was blind but now I see!"*** (John 9:25)

The details of this story left me with one distinct question: what was the significance of the mud? It baffled me that Jesus did not heal the blind man instantly. Spitting on the ground was a strange thing to do. Jesus putting mud on the blind man's eyes was uncommon, but it stirred me. The Healer's hands touched the exact point of pain. Jesus zeroed-in on the problem. These impressions were taking form within my imagination as I sat in my recliner. I couldn't shake the story.

> *I don't understand much about this story. I am curious, like the disciples. I wish I could just have a talk with Jesus right now and ask a few questions.*

The scenario of the past week played over in my mind like a movie. I recalled the euphoria of discovering *Psalm 119:116*. Only a few days later the bottom fell out. Doubt opened the door and fear walked right in. By the grace of God, I revolted against that negative spirit. I absolutely would not allow it to rule me.

That poor blind man; all he wanted was his sight. But, Jesus required him to go to the pool and wash. He was such a brave soul and he immediately obeyed the Master. Consequently, he made it to the pool and went on his way...healed.

Waiting was hard. I was becoming very weary in the drawn-out process. Emotions were running rampant and questions screamed.

Jesus, what do you want me to do? Why do I feel sorry for myself, simply because I don't have an answer? Why is everything so mysterious...so confusing? What will the outcome be?

A restless nap in the recliner did not take away the familiar heaviness of heart. I desired so much for God to show me what to do about the chemotherapy and radiation treatments. I was ticked-off at HIM for being silent.

Have you ever been in that predicament? You may as well admit it. The Lord already knows all about it.

Deep inside, I longed for a marvelous testimony of healing that would knock the socks off the entire medical community in Nashville and beyond. Some of my conversations with the Lord were somewhat comical.

God, You are really missing a golden opportunity to be lifted up in this town. Don't You know that I'm running out of time?

What a merciful God, so tenderly mindful of those human anxieties and frailties.

As a father has compassion on his children, so the Lord has compassion on those who fear him; for he knows how we are formed, he remembers that we are dust. (Psalm 103:13 & 14 - Amplified)

The ringing of the telephone interrupted my restless thoughts. On the other end of the line were our good friends, Missionaries David and Doris Godwin. These seasoned soldiers were in Mexico for another crusade. Their son, Don, had once traveled with us and played the bass guitar in our band. Our history went way back.

News of my battle with cancer had reached Mexico. We spoke briefly about the "three-month death sentence." It was odd, hearing those words come out of my mouth for the first time. We exchanged the normal niceties and I thanked them for taking time to make the call.

Then, David said, "Wait just a minute. Before we hang up, let's pray. But first, I have a little story to tell you. We believe God is going to heal you, but you may not like the way He does it this time."

Oh David! You could have left out that part about not liking the way God "does it this time."

He continued, "In the ninth book of *John* there's an interesting story of a blind man. Jesus could have healed him on the spot, but He didn't. Instead, the Lord spat on the ground and made some mud. Then he anointed the man's eyes with the mud and sent him to the pool. I can't tell you why it happened that way. Wish I could. In the end, he got his sight and God was glorified."

David and Doris prayed a short prayer and the conversation ended.

There I was in Nashville, sitting in my chair with my Bible opened to that very scripture. The phone call was not mere coincidence; David's reference to *John 9* was a divine appointment. God spoke to me in an unexpected way. Oh yes, He heard my cry. By His mercy, He prompted someone in Mexico to call. Doesn't God often surprise us in the way our prayers are answered? Indeed, the answer to my question became obvious. It was time to be still and listen.

How could I be ticked at such an awesome God? I would no longer question the timing of the Creator of the Universe. But still, there were things about the actual story that I wanted to know. What was the significance of the mud? Revelation gradually dawned in my clouded spirit. The understanding that God gave was profound and undeniable.

Mud was all the messy stuff I did not want to encounter. It was the cancer, the inconvenience, the treatments, the pain, even the mocking humiliation. The obvious losses and those yet to be suffered were part of the mud. Deeper insight would come in due time; nevertheless, it was already shining like Heavenly sunshine on the mud of my confusion. The darkened corners of my spirit were growing brighter, and the scriptures that were written thousands of years ago were illumining my soul. The mud was not a dark mystery anymore. Absolutely not! I was *created* from mud. I had even been *protected* by mud. The mud of life was all around me. Better still, the mud no longer frightened me. The washing of the Word cleanses it every time. Mud kills only when one stops moving through it. I would never give up and allow it to overwhelm me. I made a conscious decision to embrace the mud.

Insight about the mud was right on time. It was revealed to me by the phone call and the way God spoke to me earlier that day through His Word. Most of all, I was enveloped by the sweetest peace I have ever known. I surrendered to His will, although it meant going through chemotherapy and radiation. Nothing had changed, except my obedience.

When standing at the crossroads, seek the will of God. No one can tell another individual how to respond to chronic illness. I don't give advice. My desire is to simply offer hope...and faith. Hope and faith supersede medical science. God is not limited by medicine, nor is He dependent upon it.

I finally understood what the mud was all about. My decision was to go forward with treatments in peace and reclaimed assurance. All He required of me was obedience.

When Levoy returned home, he found his wife with a new mindset. My first words were, "I'm ready to get started on those treatments."

His jaw dropped in total disbelief. He had a question: "What in the world happened to you?"

I detailed the fascinating scenario about the phone call from the Godwin's and about my Bible being opened to the exact chapter. I also confessed my frustration with waiting on God.

Quickly, before I could rethink, I dialed the number. "Hello, my name is Nelva C. Dewey. You guys load up your biggest guns. I'm ready now."

I thanked God for the telephone call that reminded me of a man called Jesus and a miracle that involved some mud. Jesus reached into the mud of my circumstance with His nail-scarred hands and got involved with my mud.

Life is full of contradictions. A flood is horrific, while a cool rain on a summer day is refreshing. A fierce wind is destructive, while a gentle breeze is pleasant. The same sun that melts the snow hardens the mud. The obstacle of cancer had created horrendous mud, but a cleansing pool was waiting.

The scary West Texas storms I experienced as a small child are unforgettable. The little cattle town of Lamesa was home to about 6,500 mostly good folks, built against a backdrop of open skies, with tumbleweeds blowing across the prairie. I became accustomed to the twisters that descended on the high plains and, in a strange way, I was addicted to the excitement that accompanied them. I've seen tornados drop out of the sky suddenly, without warning. The atmosphere would be eerily transformed beneath a black, boiling sky. No public warning system was in place to alert those in harm's way of the dangerous weather. We sought shelter from the terror of the insidious funnels that marched their unspeakable destruction across the plains, in the safe haven of Papa's earthen cellar across the street. I can still close my eyes and feel those worn dirt steps on my backside as I slid downward into the cool musty earth.

There have been times when dark clouds blocked the light of hope. The same storms that assail your life, assail mine. The adversary will never lie down and forget about the seeker who is following hard after God.

The more committed one becomes for the cause of Christ, the more intense the opposition.

With each advance we made in the ministry, we felt the sting of hostile winds. They blew upon us, but they did not blow us off course. We persevered through financial deficit and discouragement. Advancements were made and triumphs were celebrated in spite of the difficulties.

Victories never come without conflict. There is a place on the top of each mountain where the sun is shining. One never rises to the next level without experiencing the struggle of the climb.

Living on a mountain top, exempt from the struggles of life and its difficulties, may never happen. Yet, the sweetest flowers bloom in the deep valley shadows. Their fragrance long reminds the sojourners of God's sustaining grace during the pressing trials.

In our travels, I've been awed by the fascinating palm trees along the coasts. Their flexible trunks bend down to the ground as they're hammered by the seasonal hurricanes and cyclones. These mighty trees are extremely resilient and their leaves remain green year round. The palm trees withstand because of their deep roots. Though tossed about and brought low, they are seldom destroyed. On calm days they stand tall, proudly bearing the scars of past tempests, ready to face yet another storm.

When the storm of terminal illness struck my world, it was not possible to run to Papa's dirt cellar. My shelter was under the wings of the Almighty. The faith that had sustained me since childhood had grown deep roots. Like those mighty palm trees, I had been conditioned to stand. My physical body and emotions would suffer a storm that I never dreamed possible one day before it hit. Somehow, I saw the next chapters of my life like the palm trees.

He shall be like a tree planted by the rivers of water that brings forth its fruit in its season.
(Psalm 1:3 - NKJV)

It takes a storm to know your strength. It also takes a storm to know your weakness.

The tree that's planted by the water is unmovable. Truly, the water of the Word is the source of strength in my life.

By God's grace I would rise above the storm.

P **R** *A Y E R*

RISE!

The eagle spreads its mighty wings and rides upon the storm to lofty heights.

An old cliché says, "It's impossible to fly like an eagle if you think like a turkey!" Your thoughts determine what you will accomplish in life. Your success in navigating the storms depends upon your ability to get on top of the obstacles along the way.

For as he thinks in his heart, so is he...
(Proverbs 23:7 - NKJV)

The bald eagle's keen instincts warn him of the coming storm. This amazing bird, sensing peril in the atmosphere, strategically positions himself on top of the storm and allows its thrust to raise him high above the danger. He doesn't need to struggle. The sun is always shining on top of the clouds.

The secret to rising *above* the storm is resting *in* the storm.

...those who wait on the Lord shall renew their strength; they shall mount up with wings like

eagles, they shall run and not be weary, they shall walk and not faint. (Isaiah 40:31 - NKJV)

PRAYER: *Lord Jesus, You are in the midst of every storm. I am depending on You like never before. Forgive me for ever doubting You. I long for the time when I am safe and looking down upon the dark clouds that You brought me through. Help me soar on wings of faith to a new level.* AMEN.

3

Ask
with Confidence

*T*ennessee is breathtaking in the fall. It is the season I have always loved best. Something quickens in my senses at the first descent of falling leaves and the little nip in the air. When the trees that adorn the rolling hills make their colorful announcement of the new season, the city of Nashville is truly picturesque.

Autumn was different that year. The threat of terminal illness was distracting, as the issues of life and thoughts of dying consumed me. Chemotherapy and radiation treatments started in October. When I walked into the treatment room at the Frist Building for the first time, and saw all the patients hooked up to IV's in the infusion room, it really hit hard. I had a flashback of first grade, when we stood in a straight line, waiting for our shots. Some kids were crying in fear of the needle. One little girl, who also wanted to cry, did not; instead, she consoled the others. The six year-old bravely assured each one, "Don't be scared, it won't hurt...promise." She wittingly stepped behind each classmate, one by one. At last, her eyes scanned the room. She was standing alone at the end of the line. It was her turn and she felt sick to her stomach.

As the needle sank into her taut little arm, the blood drained from her face and her body hit the floor like a rock. When she opened her eyes the school nurse was still in shock. "I cannot believe Cleon fainted. She was so brave, and she was comforting all the others."

Now the same scene played out in a large room full of cancer patients, each waiting our turn. We all were in the same boat on a rolling sea of uncertainty. Some were visibly shaken. Once again, I wanted to cry; instead, I squared my shoulders, took a deep breath and braced myself for the dreaded needles of chemotherapy.

The mud of treatments began. This time, the little girl did not faint.

No, this was not what I had wanted. Not what I expected. Then I remembered David's prayer of *Psalm 119:116*. In an instant I recalled a time and place only a few weeks ago, although it seemed like another lifetime. I reversed quickly back to the bedroom when I saw the Bible verse. It was not only the Psalmist's supplication; it was mine. I asked God to uphold me, according to His promise and let me not be ashamed in my hope. Deep in the mud, the seed of God's Word was germinating. By faith, I knew it was there, growing and changing.

The sounds of the treatment room brought me back to the present. I hoped that my fellow patients carried within their hearts the light of hope into the unknown darkness of their personal storms. Something more promising than anything chemo-therapy or radiation offered was needed; each of us needed faith in an unfailing God. I breathed a prayer of compassion for all those suffering the pangs of disease.

God, please give an encouraging word to someone who needs it today. Someone who is hurting, like me.

Time seemed to become stuck in a monotonous pattern of treatment for two week periods, followed by two weeks of rest. Chemo caused almost constant nausea and the taste of chemicals in my mouth was putrid. A strange odor lingered in my nostrils long after the IV's were finished. The very thought of food was repulsive.

Immediately after the four-hour infusions, I made my way across the street to Baptist Hospital for radiation. The first two treatments were unremarkable, and I was encouraged. Then it hit: a relentless, burning pain of caustic sores from radiation. There was no place to hide and no relief. Even the prescription ointment that was supposed to ease the pain was ineffective. Every day presented another reason to cry.

Believe it or not, there were even reasons to laugh. With the discomfort of blisters that had begun to appear on my underside, I felt the need for a small fan to sit on the bed that would direct cool air where I needed it most. I decided to dash over to the store closest to our home. I quickly located the fan, tossed it into a shopping basket and was making my way to the check-out counter when it hit...like a tsunami. The merciless effects of chemo and radiation collided like a fury in my digestive tract. Without warning, hot, liquid diarrhea cascaded down my legs. Thankfully, I was wearing dark slacks!

Something arose within my stubborn will.

I will not be denied the relief of that fan...no matter what!

My steps quickened, along with everything else. The home goods department was down the next isle. I grabbed the thickest towel on the shelf and made a dash for the cashier, knowing that my car seat would thank me. The other customers in line looked all around, with searching noses held high. The origin of the foul smell that wafted through the store was a mystery to all. I mirrored their wondering glances and put on a convincing frown of curiosity. That was my last shopping trip for a very long time.

Back at the house, the clothes went into the washing machine and I jumped into a warm shower, trying to cleanse my thoughts as well as my body of the horrendous episode. The positive aspect of the incident was the realization that I could keep my cool. Renewed confidence that I would make it through *any* humiliation was my reward. Not only did I make it; I found humor in the experience.

God orchestrates the chronology of events when we surrender everything to Him. He puts exactly the right components in place in times of crisis, including special individuals who bring laughter. People have diverse personalities and various gifts that are invaluable.

Sharon Metzgar has been in my life for a long time. Her parents were in my mother's Sunday school class for teenagers in Lamesa, Texas. Sharon was by my side during the most crucial episodes of my life. The day I got "marked" for radiation treatments, Sharon and my daughter, Cindy, accompanied me to Baptist Hospital. The marks were strategically placed and remained on my body throughout treatment, as indicators for the radiologist. Part of the process required placing a little flag in the flesh of my behind. I lay quietly on my tummy, trying to be very, very still. The flag had to stay upright; it could not move even a tiny bit.

I turned my head just enough to see through the glass window. Sharon stood erect, with her hand held over her heart, and her eyes glued to the precariously positioned flag. I could see her lips moving as she recited the Pledge of Allegiance. The impulsive display of comedy did not escape the keen eyes of the radiologist. When a doctor laughs during such a tedious task, it has to be really funny.

Two weeks on and two weeks off; the calendar was marked and the days were counted off, as I anticipated the reprieve. The long awaited weeks of rest could not come soon enough. Treatments were nearly intolerable. How often I considered the steps of the blind man over whose eyes Jesus put the mud He made. The blind man made it to the pool and so would I. Had it not been for the beautiful things called "hope" and "faith," I would have despaired.

Toward the end of each 14-day rest, I started feeling better. The nausea and burning subsided. Some say the mind cannot recall certain pain. It's true; otherwise, no woman would have more than one baby. Likewise, without that blissful absence of memory, continuing with treatments would have been impossible. Too soon, it was time to start another cycle. Determination took over and I went back for the next round of "chemo-mud."

The sheer dread of more chemicals and radiation sores was depressing. Knowing the dark cloud would eventually pass kept me moving forward. Clinging to the promises, now embedded in my core, kept my faith intact.

> **For I will restore health to you and heal you of your wounds, says the Lord...**
>
> (Jeremiah 30:17 – NKJV)

The Bible does not promise an easy road, but God will bring restoration no matter how bad the situation. I found my strength in the Word that promised that my wounds would be healed. Doubt may have clouded my early decision making about treatment, but I never doubted God's power. I was grateful for Oncologist Karl Rogers and all the help that medical knowledge offered, but my confidence did not rest in medicine...never did.

The reasons for complying with doctors' orders were twofold: first, I knew that God could use medicine, like Jesus used the mud in *John 9*; second, I was on a mission of obedience. The outcome was not my responsibility. When faith is released, confidence takes over.

Everyone in the hospitals and clinics I entered, from the receptionists' desks to the back door, heard about Jesus' healing a blind man in John's Gospel. Those precious, hurting souls in the confines of treatment rooms were my captive audience. I never knew so much sickness existed in one little city. Some of the sick had never heard Jesus' healing stories. Others knew the stories, but believed they were no more than ancient fables. Other patients encouraged me, brightened my day and showed me how sustaining a positive word can be.

Once I met my new "chemotherapy friends," self-pity was out the door. I empathized with those who did not believe that miracles are for us today. How does one survive such storms without faith in God? Each time I shared my testimony, my faith grew a little more. Confession with the mouth strengthens one's resolve to persevere. Realizing the power of the spoken word ignited my fire. I made a conscious habit of audibly speaking prayers, no matter where I happened to be. Onlookers probably thought I was talking to myself. Time after time, I declared that God had heard and the answer was on the way. I worshipped my Creator for who He is, and I praised Him for bending low to hear and answer my prayers.

...they overcame him (Satan) by the blood of the
Lamb and by the word of their testimony, and they
did not love their lives to the death.

(Revelation 12:11 - NKJV)

If you need to be delivered or healed, spend
some time visiting a hospital. Your focus will soon
be fixed on the needs of other people. Find
someone else to encourage and your own
problems will be diminished.

While sitting on cold, vinyl chairs of various waiting rooms, I thought a lot about the mud. My goal was reaching that pool. The greatest challenge was keeping my mind focused on positive things. Knowing that God always provides a way of escape gave me hope for a better day.

Dwelling on the pain of the present destroys
confidence.

Soon, I would hear my name, "Nelva Dewey." Just about the only time I've ever heard "Nelva" was in a doctor's office or a hospital. I smiled and made a mental note.

I must remember to remove my first name from
everything, unless it is required by law. Mother, I
forgive you for the name thing.

At times I felt like I was in a horror movie. I was the muddy figure, moving through the shadows. There must have been sunlight to create the shadows, but it could not be seen. The pool was far away, but one day it would surely come into view. Like the blind man, the infirm, belabored soul refused to die in the darkness.

Chemical infusions entered my body, but it was the living Word that was restoring my health.

Lord, I will not be afraid to face the needles and the burns. Protect me from harm. Let the bad cells die. Protect the good ones.

In my heart of hearts, I knew the Lord would not send me on a pointless journey. I was His chosen, not a character in a sadistic plot. Beneath the cumbersome mud of cancer, an ember of hope still burned deep within my spirit. No doubt about it, the healing waters would be transforming. God's timing was the only uncertainty. The hardest part was to keep moving in the right direction, to keep believing and not despair. Deliverance, sweet deliverance would be glorious!

Riding home in the car after treatments, Cindy sang her heart out, praising the Lord. The enemy had to leave. Praise is always appropriate and it confuses the enemy. The door to victory opens a little wider with every utterance of praise.

I will offer to You the sacrifice of thanksgiving,
and I will call upon the name of the Lord.

(Psalm 116:17 - NKJV)

Spiritual battles are fought and won through prayer. The Word says to give thanks...always. It is a full time job to keep a spirit of gratitude in the midst of mud.

Rejoice always, Pray without ceasing, In
everything give thanks; for this is the will of God in
Christ Jesus for you. Do not quench the Spirit. Do
not despise prophecies.

(II Thessalonians 5:16-20 - NKJV)

At home, Suzanne and Nathan continued speaking into existence those things not yet seen. Our children are "praise activists" and have learned the value of praise in spiritual warfare. Cancer did not quiet their tongues or stifle their songs. The atmosphere was constantly charged with positive confession. Thanksgiving to God opens the floodgates of Heaven and ushers us into His presence. Suzanne and Nathan went often to soul-stirring services that renewed their hope and fortified their faith. The anointing that breaks the yoke of bondage was working. When they returned to the house, I heard their strong confessions and songs of triumph. The bondage of fear was broken again and again. Many times they rejoiced around my bed, thanking God for resurrecting their mother from the death of cancer. They asked with confidence for a miracle.

> *Let us hold fast the confession of our hope without wavering, for He who promised is faithful.*
> (Hebrews 10:23 - NKJV)

> *Sing to the Lord with thanksgiving; Sing praises on the harp to our God, Who covers the heavens with clouds, Who prepares rain for the earth, Who makes grass to grow on the mountains.*
> (Psalm 7:7-8 - NKJV)

Abraham had a promise from God that he would be the father of many nations. The promise appeared to be impossible, yet he believed. Sarah was too old to bear children. God is not moved by physical facts. He is moved by the truth of His promise.

> *Yet he [Abraham] did not waver through unbelief regarding the promise of God, but was strengthened in his faith and gave glory to God, being fully persuaded that God had power to do what he had promised.* (Romans 4:20 - NIV)

At long last, chemotherapy and radiation treatments were finished...no more nausea. The blisters dried. Slowly, my strength returned. Radiation had burned all of the tissue in its path. They warned me that I would sustain scarring both inside and out. The lingering side-effects of chemotherapy would be devastating. I was also warned that my immune system would be shut down. This would make me susceptible to every communicable disease that came around. I quickly cleared my head of those predictions and made no plans to make them come true. The prognosis did not agree with the promise buried in my heart. The positive confession of my mouth was the antidote to the negative forecast.

My strength is being renewed by the power of the living God and I will come out of this in great victory. I will be cancer-free!

The next MRI showed that the tumor had shrunk from the size of a tennis ball to that of a quarter. What a drastic difference! We rejoiced for the good report. Things were looking brighter. My hope surged high. I could see a bright light at the end of the dark tunnel, and it was not an oncoming train. I concluded that surgery would not be necessary.

Routine tests were scheduled to determine the outcome of treatments more accurately. Those harrowing months of October and November would never be forgotten. I had seen enough mud to last a mighty long time.

Levoy took me to lunch for the first time in many weeks. It felt good to do something normal, like getting dressed and going out again. My appointment was scheduled with Dr. Fisher that afternoon. I anticipated no more bad news.

The doctor did a biopsy in his clinic. It was a simple procedure, called a probe, to check the area for cancer cells. I was already upbeat because of the recent MRI. I noticed that Dr. Fisher was a bit reserved. He didn't appear to be ready to congratulate me just yet, but I didn't give it much thought.

Doctors are funny that way. He will give me a clean bill of health when he gets the results from the probe.

The next morning the call came from Dr. Fisher's office. A female voice asked to speak to Nelva. "The test showed no signs of cancer." I was elated beyond measure to hear those words. I screamed, "I just knew it...Hallelujah!" Still holding the phone, I jumped for joy around the kitchen. Then, I realized that the conversation was not over. The kind nurse was trying to get a word in edgewise. "We think you need to hear the doctor's opinion on the probe. He believes that the possibility of missing even one lone cancer cell is too risky. You need to come in for consultation in the morning. Dr. Fisher would like to talk to you and your husband about surgery."

Euphoria was short-lived, as a bucket of cold water was dumped on my head and all my hopes were iced. I was confounded...good news...bad news. Surgery was a step I was not prepared to take. Chemotherapy and radiation had been monumental decisions, but surgery far surpassed mere treatments. That phone call knocked me down to the bottom; I felt disappointed and devastated.

For the first time, I felt angry. I complained, "So what if the tumor reduced in size! It doesn't mean a thing! They don't give a hoot about the probe being negative. All they want to do is cut on me!" I cried until I fell asleep in the wee hours of a very dark night, lying across the foot of the bed.

Levoy held me. We were in this fight together. He pleaded, "Please, Honey, let's go talk to the doctor. He knows more than we know. Let's go for it. Remember, it's just more mud."

The next morning, Levoy set up the consultation. I did not know what was going to happen, but I was finished with being angry. The words of a song we wrote and recorded had brand new meaning:

> *"I'd rather live by faith than try to make it on feelings; I'd rather trust in God than count on my own dealings; The Word of God will never change, but feelings get rearranged; I'd rather live by faith than try to make it on feelings."*

In his no-sugar-coated manner, Dr. Fisher methodically delivered the next blow. "Surgery is an absolute necessity. No question about it. It is the next and final step in the treatment process." He reiterated, "The real possibility of missing one cancer cell hanging out in there is playing Russian roulette with your life."

At that moment, I saw a tender side of the man. Gently patting my hand, he reminded me of my potential for long life and the probability of a very good outcome. The surgery would secure a better chance for longevity...time with my husband...our children...the grandchildren.

A statement I had made in times past was, "The worst thing in the world would be blindness." Isn't it interesting that the story of a blind man impressed me so much? But that was only the first half of my statement. "The next worst thing," I would continue, "would be a colostomy." There, in Dr. Fisher's office, I faced the second worse pronouncement I could imagine. If blindness was not a problem to the Healer, neither was a colostomy.

It was time for some serious soul searching. Three beautiful grandchildren held my heart. Cindy and Mark's six year-old Rachel, and one year-old Daniel, were our first two grandchildren. Suzanne and Nathan's son, Elijah, was our third grandbaby. Daniel was the first male to be born on the Cotton side of the family in 53 years. My brother, Clois, had five daughters. Those daughters had given him and Nancy six granddaughters. Most definitely, my side of the family was proud finally to have a boy in the mix. With the hope of more babies yet to be added to our growing family, I had compelling reasons to fight. Grandchildren bring such joy, and I did not want to miss watching them grow and imparting into their future.

> *How could Levoy start over again without me by his side? He needed me. We had been a team in life and ministry since we were married.*

Every conceivable option was weighed, but the conclusion was clear. The fruition of plans long dreamed and the completion of God's will had not yet been fully realized. No! I would not give up. I would stake a claim for every day that God had designed for me. Death did not frighten me, but I flatly refused to be robbed of a single day. The hope of Heaven purifies. The wonders of that eternal realm are beyond comprehension, but I did not have closure on life. It was not my time to go.

In the mud I learned some things. God is far more interested in people than in things. His compassion is never more obvious than in times of loss and suffering. He chose me to be His hand extended, as an answer to someone *else's* prayer. I met many sick people within a short time and their stories are still fresh. Whether healing came in this present world or on the other side was not my call to make. I simply shared my faith and left the outcome in God's hands. My "inconvenience" seemed insignificant when weighed in the balance of His purpose. That was a liberating thought.

The fight was on...big time. I rejected the option of sitting down in the mud and dying! Submitting to a surgery that would change the rest of my life, however, was the hardest decision I had ever faced. I picked up a pen and thoughtfully, with trembling hands, signed the consent paper.

A deep awareness had settled upon me. My heart knew that God had entrusted me to bear special scars. Somehow, He would turn the scars into stars. I could not afford to fail Him. That is when I began to comprehend the great responsibility that was upon me. Could God trust me with that much mud? That is why I trembled.

The evening before surgery, Levoy and all the family were gathered in the hospital room. We prayed together, and my resolve was strengthened in those private moments. It was a small window of time to reassure my loved ones that I was strong in spirit and ready to get on with this "crazy" surgery. Talking about it was therapeutic. Our thoughts were jammed with questions that found expression; questions that only time could answer. I did not fully understand all the "whys," but there is perfect peace in surrender.

There was a folder on the table, filled with graphic descriptions of a typical colostomy, or simply, an "ostomy." There were various pictures of "stomas," depicting the opening that connected the bowel to the outside of the body. The information was intended to prepare the patient for the way in which they would soon be caring for bodily functions. Coming face-to-face with this stark reality might typically have been a sober moment. However, the girls found comedy in the ghastly images that were depicted. I was amused. We all knew the seriousness, but it was time to lighten up. Nothing soothes my soul and relieves stress like the warmth of my children's voices. Humor is a little wink from God, assuring that all is well.

Dr. Fisher opened the door slowly and entered with a degree of caution. He motioned for Mother to join him in the hall. Perhaps he considered her the only sane person in the room. His concern was phrased in a question: "Does your daughter understand the seriousness of what she's facing?"

Without hesitation, Mother replied, "Yes, she's had her tears. She knows."

The best witness in a sad world is a joyful heart. Joy is a by-product of peace. It was not unthinkable to laugh in the face of a major surgery. I was taken aback by the circumstance I faced, of course, but the decision was already made and reconciled in my spirit. Praying through made the difference.

A cheerful heart is good medicine, but a crushed spirit dries up the bones. (Proverbs 17:22 - NIV)

When Mother and the doctor reentered the room, I consoled him, "I have faith in God for a good outcome of surgery. I feel confident in your abilities, Dr. Fisher. I also know that you can do nothing without God's help, so I am asking Him to guide your hands as you do your job."

He responded politely, "A positive attitude is a good thing."

Trying to avoid the ring of arrogance, I said, "It's more than a positive attitude. It's faith in God."

Patting my shoulder, Dr. Fisher said, "I like that." As he turned to leave, he shrugged his shoulders and said, "Whatever works for you."

I knew Dr. Fisher was a skilled physician and respected in his field. Yet, in spite of his knowledge, the brilliant professional, with the highly trained mind and skilled hands, did not comprehend my confidence in prayer. My calm assurance in Almighty God eluded his understanding, yet he was intrigued. Oh, how I longed for my surgeon to see the power of God manifested in me.

Three days later, Dr. Fisher bounced into my hospital room with a really big smile on his face. He had the results from the pathologist and was ready to pass along the latest information. Mother and I were eagerly waiting for the report and we hung on his every word. He explained, "Tissue that was removed in surgery was positive for cancer. Aren't you glad we got that thing out of there? Now, we're reasonably certain all the cancerous cells were removed, but there's never a guarantee. The lesion reduced in size even more than we first thought, to the size of a raisin. As you already know, two and a half feet of your colon have been removed. You can live without that, right? Your internal organs look great, including the liver."

Then he looked directly into my eyes and smiled. "It works for you!" He knew that I knew what "it" was. He had seen the power of prayer.

I have heard it said, "There are three ways to fight cancer: poison, burn and cut." The most effective weapon is missing from that list: Prayer! Prayer changes everything.

I shared the report with Levoy when he arrived at the hospital later in the morning. He was surprised that so much of my colon was gone; two and a half feet! With a sly grin on his face, Levoy asked, "Does that mean I can call you...'semi-colon?'"

I laughed so hard, I worried the stitches would pop. "Yes," I said, "but only this one time; never again!"

You may wonder how I could ride so high one minute and plummet to the bottom the next. I have a simple answer: I am a human being, bound in mortal flesh, who sometimes errs by looking at circumstances. I am also a spiritual being, in whom the unfailing Word resides. With God I cannot fail and neither can you!

Little children, you are of God...you belong to Him...and have [already] defeated and overcome them [agents of antichrist], because He Who lives in you is greater (mightier) than he who is in the world. (I John 4:4 - Amplified)

Mother made a decision to remain in Nashville until I was well enough to resume traveling. She patiently waited for the day when my life would return to normal. That would be the day when I was able to step on the bus and roll toward another service with Levoy.

Our local church's ministry was a tremendous blessing. The messages of the pastor were recorded and made available every week. Women in the congregation brought meals to our home to nourish the physical needs of our family.

It is vital for the body of Christ to be proactive in helping one another. Those who commit themselves to outreach ministries are shining beacons of light. The countless hands that touched our lives are deeply appreciated.

When I expressed concern about how the surgery would change my life, Dr. Fisher assured me. "Continue performing your normal activities. You can still do anything you think you can do." I like to think big and those challenging words were music to my ears. The following weeks were laced with many complications. Learning a new way of handling bodily functions was frustrating and the adjustments were not easy. My new routine was awkward, but stubborn determination arose with each new obstacle. My comfort level increased day by day, and a sense of well-being soon returned.

January 4, 1995 was a milestone. For the first time in four months, I packed my suitcases, boarded our converted Eagle bus and headed toward Florida with my happy husband. Yes! I was back in the swing of ministry and there was no looking back.

My grateful Mother boarded a plane and flew home to Amarillo the next day. God had answered her prayers.

The predictions by many doctors, of failing strength and overall health problems following chemotherapy and radiation, never happened. I did not catch colds, suffer flu or chronic fatigue. My strength returned, along with the good health that I had enjoyed before the storm of cancer. God was not finished with me yet.

Another miracle out of the mud was that I had experienced no back pain since the surgery. For several years prior to cancer, I had severe backaches. Soon after returning from the hospital, I realized that my back was strong. The attacks that debilitated me previously were history.

Mud changes people. It changed me. In the midnight hour, I made a promise to God:

Deliver me from this cancer and I will testify for Your honor and glory...anywhere...anytime.

This is one of the wonderful psalms that sustained me through the stages of recovery. It never fails to encourage and inspire, time after time:

Though I walk in the midst of trouble, Thou wilt revive me: thou shalt stretch forth thine hand against the wrath of mine enemies, and thy right hand shall save me. The Lord will perfect that which concerneth me: thy mercy, O Lord, endureth for ever: forsake not the works of thine own hands.
(Psalm 138:7&8 - KJV)

The perfecting process is not a rosy path. Ask the blind man. Ask the patriarchs, who withstood fiery trials, flood, peril, shipwreck, persecution and prison. They had one thing in common: every one of them went through a rigorous process of being perfected. Seasons of perfecting are common to us all. I call them *"mudding."* Be assured, God will honor His promises and perfect that which concerns His own. Just as He had mercy for them, He has mercy for you and me.

This I recall to my mind, therefore I have hope. Through the Lord's mercies we are not consumed, because His compassions fail not. They are new every morning; great is Your faithfulness.
(Lamentations 3:21-23 - NKJV)

Cancer threatened my life. It also threatened the existence of our ministry. I had been homebound for four months. Levoy persevered. He gritted it out, dug deep and made good on the dates for ministry that were booked. On a few occasions, Nathan traveled with him. Regretfully, it wasn't always feasible to take our son-in-law away from his recording work and his obligations at the church where he was on staff. Many engagements were cancelled, because Levoy needed to be with me. The schedule for services waned and resulted in loss of income.

The day we resumed traveling was a major turnaround. My husband had his "side-kick" once again. By God's grace, we would reclaim every inch of ground the enemy had taken from us.

...Pursue: for thou shalt surely overtake them, and without fail recover all. (I Samuel 30:8 - KJV)

Audiences met us with enthusiasm. They were encouraged to hear about a blind man, who went through the mud and received his sight at the pool. *John 9* was a relevant story that challenged them to have courage in their mud of life.

Public speaking was something to which I never aspired. Before cancer, it took an act of congress to get a simple testimony out of me. I wrote songs, played the keyboard and rarely missed a service, but most of my work was behind the scenes, just the way I liked it. I thought I had struck the perfect balance, within the box of my comfort zone. After all, actions speak louder than words, right?

Cancer had not stopped me, and had placed very few limitations on me. Some pastors were surprised when I stepped up to the microphone to speak. It was a new day, and one that was blessed.

> *The spirit of the Lord God is upon me, because the Lord has anointed me to preach good tidings to the poor; He has sent me to heal the brokenhearted, to proclaim liberty to the captives, and the opening of the prison to those who are bound. To proclaim the acceptable year of the Lord, and the day of vengeance of our God; To comfort all who mourn; To console those who mourn in Zion, to give them beauty for ashes, the oil of joy for mourning, the garment of praise for the spirit of heaviness.* (Isaiah 61:1-3 - NKJV)

We ministered in many churches across the country. After sharing my heart, I prayed for people at the conclusion of every service. The mantle that rested upon me was humbling, and the sobering story of how it passed to me will never be forgotten. I survived the storm and made it through the mud.

For the next eight years, my life was crowned by God's goodness and mercy. Levoy and I were also blessed by the birth of two more grandchildren, two more reasons to live. Andrew Larson and Benjamin Young, both wonderfully amazing boys, were added to the quiver.

The five year mark is significant in cancer recovery. In most cases the disease does not return after that point. Every cancer patient watches the calendar with a degree of anticipation. There is a long-awaited sigh of relief when one reaches the five-year mark with no recurrence of the disease. Higher percentages for long life and wellness are expected from that time forward. It was no different for me. It was a red letter day and I wanted to shout it to the whole world: "Good news! It's been five years! I am cancer free!"

I gained deeper understanding, having walked through the mud of cancer. The scars healed and I embraced my new reality with a grateful heart. I shared the testimony, ministering and praying for people.

Joy comes in the morning light. The season of mourning was gone. The Lord was my safe anchor through the dark storm of cancer. It was in those lonely, midnight hours that I found courage in God's unfailing Word to pray with confidence.

When the episode of cancer was written, I never imagined a sequel. Recurring cancer never entered my mind. The mud of cancer was past.

Or was it?

P R A Y E R

ASK!

"The ones who ask with confidence know the heart of the giver."

A busy pastor, stressed with the cares of life and needing a quiet place to prepare for Sunday's sermon, retreated to his secluded attic study. Before ascending to his private hideaway he announced that he would tolerate no interruptions. He was just getting settled when a persistent knock broke the silence. Who would have the nerve? He shoved his chair back and threw the door open. There stood his five year-old daughter, looking up into her father's eyes. She said, "Daddy, you have been so busy. I didn't have a chance to say, 'I love you.'" Instinctively, his big arms embraced his little girl. All tension vanished in one tender moment. The contented child skipped away. At last, he knelt to pray.

"Lord, please forgive me. I've been so busy. I just want to tell you that 'I love You.'"

Spending time with the Father makes everything right.

Because he has set his love upon Me...I will deliver him...He shall call upon me and I will answer him; I will be with him in trouble; I will deliver him and honor him. With long life I will satisfy him, and show him my salvation.

(Psalm 14:14-16 - NKJV)

I love those who love me, and those who seek me diligently will find me. (Proverbs 8:17 - NKJV)

PRAYER: *Blessed Savior, thank you for loving me in spite of my faults. Sometimes I can't imagine why You chose me. I want You to be pleased with me. Your love has never failed. It has brought me through every trial. I will seek You; I will serve You; I will love You with more passion. Give me a heart of compassion. Amen.*

4

Yield
to His Presence

*W*e moved Mother to Nashville, following her first stroke. She left the home where she had spent the last years with Daddy. Everything she had accumulated was sorted and many items discarded. My brother and his wife helped with the details and I flew to Amarillo to drive her car to Tennessee. Her new living quarters were set up in the lower level of our home.

Before departing the house that held so many memories, we paused to remember. The picture was branded in my memory: Mother and Daddy enjoying their breakfast at the kitchen table by the big window, entertained by their feathered and furry friends as they scampered about the yard and flitted through the trees. After Daddy passed away, Mother sat alone by the window. The August morning was unusually still, as if the squirrels and birds were offering a moment of silence, in honor of their audience of one.

We cherished Mother's presence in our home. Her godly wisdom had a calming effect on others. For about three years, she required little assistance. As Levoy and I maintained our traveling schedule and were out of town much of the time, Mother drove her car around a small radius in the neighborhood and enjoyed limited independence. Our daughters lived close by and were available when she needed them.

When Mother suffered a second stroke suddenly, we could no longer come and go at will and she required a watchful eye. I started sleeping on a couch near her bedroom. She was alert and noticed that I visited the restroom frequently throughout the night. I waved off her concerns with a list of excuses, and reminded her that I was taking antibiotics for a bladder infection. Everything would be fine, I declared, once the problem cleared up. At the same time, I was having unsettling thoughts of my own. Her intuition had been correct when I had cancer before and it was she who coaxed me to see the doctor. I was extremely tired. I hoped—oh, how I hoped—that my fatigue was due to lack of rest and nothing more serious.

A red flag went up the day I called Dr. Anderson for a fourth antibiotic prescription. A glance into my folder prompted his response: "That's too much for six months." He insisted that I book an appointment at his hospital office. After reviewing the lab work he sent me to see the urologist. The bladder probe was negative and it showed no abnormality. That finding was a mixed blessing. Although I was relieved, there was still no answer for the chronic bladder infection.

Christmas holidays were approaching; it was certainly not a good time to be distracted by doctors' appointments. Cindy and Suzanne were making plans, many of which included my involvement. Shopping had to be done; there would be gifts to wrap and bag; all of the usual decorating, baking, planning meals, and countless details were looming.

Activities that normally bring so much pleasure were a struggle. I am not a person who gives in to fatigue, but keeping up the pace was nearly impossible. Pain worsened every day and my strength was depleted. I was trying, unsuccessfully, with all my might to catch the rhythm of the season.

The doctor's appointment, scheduled two days after Christmas, hung over my head like a low ceiling. Recurring cancer was the furthest suspicion from my mind. I quickly canceled any thought of such a possibility and kicked myself for allowing this bothersome issue to interfere with the holidays.

Who ever heard of having a doctor's appointment two days after Christmas? I already had cancer. I made it to the pool! Cancer, and all the mud that went with it, is history.

On December 27, 2002, Levoy and I sat in Dr. Anderson's office. After reviewing the negative results of the bladder probe, my doctor did not retreat. He was even more convinced that my symptoms indicated something more problematic. The source of the infection was still a mystery. He ordered a pelvic MRI, all the while making an attempt to prepare me for the worst. "I am so sorry, but this looks like cancer."

Once again, that cold word. I could not wrap my brain around the possibility of more cancer.

What is the doctor talking about? It is ludicrous to think these bladder infections could have anything to do with cancer. No way!

Then I remembered the blind man in *John 9*. Jesus did not promise him there would be no more mud, ever again, once he was healed. I concluded that as long as life continues, there will be mud.

We enthusiastically told Dr. Anderson about our plans for spending the New Year's holiday in Florida. We were emphatic that nothing would interfere with our plans. The doctor said that the MRI results would be reviewed before we left town.

The MRI was done the next morning at the Imaging Center. Levoy and I were back in Dr. Anderson's office for consultation that afternoon. He was taking a closer look at the radiologist's report when we entered the room. On his face was a look of apprehension I had never seen before. Immediately, we knew that the findings were not favorable. The doctor's attempt to be positive did not fool me; it was too soon for a prognosis, but we clearly perceived his concern.

Dr. Anderson said, "I think you are facing an uphill battle with this thing. The MRI confirms my first impression. I believe the best way to go is to see a gynecologist who specializes in difficult cases. I'll do some checking and get back with you the first week in January. For now, forget all this and enjoy your family. Have a nice trip."

His comments carried a tone of fatalism. Forget about cancer? That was impossible!

The Christmas holidays came and went far too quickly. Cindy's husband, Mark, had relatives in town from cities around the United States and parts of Central America. Both of Mark's sisters and their husbands are involved in world missions. Larry and Melodee Gruetzmacher were serving in Mexico.

Jason and Cindee Frenn were conducting crusades in Costa Rica at the time. Hearing stories of the gospel's advancement in remote places was a treat.

Seeing Larry doing so well after his own bout with cancer was inspiring. His telephone calls of encouragement, in months to come, always lifted my spirits. Hearing the voice of a cancer survivor was a gentle reminder that not everybody who faces cancer dies.

Mark's parents, Dick and Jan Larson, were the first foreign Missionaries with whom we had the opportunity of working. Our paths crossed in Panama, when they invited us to participate in a crusade. That initial experience on the mission field changed our lives. For many years, we were short-term missionary evangelists, tithing 10 percent of our time overseas and traveling to 33 countries. Panama still holds a tender place in our hearts, because it was our first missionary adventure and we returned to that "field" many times.

Sammy and Portia Young, parents of our other son-in-law, Nathan, joined us for numerous Christmas celebrations. We always looked forward to fellowship with these extended family members, and we hosted everyone for brunch before heading in different directions. We lingered for a while around the table, savoring the last moments of Christmas together. Overshadowing our gathering was news of my returning cancer. It was the "elephant in the room."

Heads were bowed in prayer before we said our goodbyes. Afterward, Jason Frenn said something to me that struck a chord. He admonished, "Don't lose sight of the hand of God."

The hand of God?

Jason's statement, while I was stuck on auto-pilot and trying to function with the "elephant" sitting on my shoulders, challenged me to see the hand of God in the unwanted surprise of recurring cancer. The impact of his words was momentous.

I searched the scriptures to be reminded of what happened in the presence of God. Wow! The burning bush was not consumed, although it was on fire. The three Hebrew children did not perish in the king's fiery furnace. Daniel was not eaten alive in the den of lions. Sarah bore Isaac at the age of ninety to fulfill God's promise. That same son was spared from the sword of sacrifice because of God's presence. Joseph was elevated from the pit to the palace and he saved the nation of Israel. In the New Testament, the water was turned to wine at the wedding feast, because the Son of God was present.

As I recalled the numerous accounts throughout the Bible, my spirit was charged with assurance. The power of His presence is the same, yesterday, today, and forever; it would literally turn my situation around. I resolved to know that He was with me, even when I could not see His hand.

This story of Jesus, walking on the sea, emphasizes a point:

Immediately He made His disciples get into the boat and go before Him to the other side, to Bethsaida, while He sent the multitude away. And when He had sent them away, He departed to the mountain to pray. Knowing when evening came, the boat was in the middle of the sea; and He was alone on the land. Then He saw them straining at rowing, for the wind was against them. Now about the fourth watch of the night He came to them, walking on the sea, and would have passed them by. And when they saw Him walking on the sea, they supposed it was a ghost, and cried out; For they all saw Him and were troubled. But immediately He talked with them and said to them, "Be of good cheer! It is I; do not be afraid." Then He went up into the boat to them, and the wind ceased. (Mark 6:45-56 - NKJV)

The moment the storm hit, something happened to the disciples. They forgot about how Jesus multiplied the loaves and fishes, a miracle He had performed that same day. They knew Jesus personally, walking and talking with Him daily. In the midst of the storm, however, the twelve disciples thought that the Son of God was a ghost. They could not have been more wrong. Jesus showed up in the midst of their problem. Fear blinded them and they simply did not recognize their Savior.

Jesus said the same thing to them that He is saying today: "Be of good cheer. Do not be afraid."

Jesus was present in my storm. My fearful heart did not feel His presence and my human eyes could not recognize the Master. Then I heard Jason Frenn's voice, speaking into my life: "Don't lose sight of the hand of God." Words cannot describe how comforting it was to see His hand. It is impossible to be aware of His presence and remain fearful. I surrendered everything to Him, including another cancer.

Jesus suffered far more as He walked upon this Earth than I could possibly comprehend. He empathizes with every sorrow known to man. Jesus' hand touched the blind man's eyes in *John 9*, and that same nail-scarred hand touched my spiritual blindness. I yielded to His presence and His peace. Why had He seemed so far away when He was there all the time?

> *Surely He has borne our grief and carried our sorrows; yet we esteemed Him stricken, smitten by God, and afflicted. But he was wounded for our transgressions, He was bruised for our iniquities; the chastisement of our peace was upon Him, and by His stripes we are healed.* (Isaiah 53:4-5 - NKJV)

A miracle waits on the other side of a storm.

My fresh eyes began to see Him in ordinary places. Perhaps it was the unexpected delay that turned into a blessing; a change of schedule that resulted in running into a friend who needed prayer; a phone call reconnecting me to someone I had not seen in a long time; a card in the mail with an encouraging scripture. Wonderful things happen in the presence of the Lord.

The grandchildren were elated with plans for the Florida trip and spending a day at Disney World. The family performed a concert on New Year's Eve and presented the music and ministry for Sunday morning services at Cypress Cathedral, with Pastors Dwight and Mary Edwards. Through the songs and spoken word, we encouraged people. No one in this world is exempt from life's difficulties...no one. The Lord touched us, even as we reached out to others.

I was enraptured by Levoy and our children's anointed music. The soothing harmonies, the lyrics of our songs that were birthed during difficult times, and the spoken Word, were a healing balm to my troubled soul.

There I was, once again, in the mud of cancer. It was an uncanny replay of eight years before. Would there be other services, more songs, or opportunities for future trips? I didn't know what tomorrow held, but I knew He would be there.

For those fleeting days, I savored every part of being together with family. My heart would ever remember that time, no matter what was on the horizon. The warm Florida sunshine was indeed a January blessing.

The hum of the diesel engine, combined with the bumping rhythm of rolling tires on the highway, was a familiar tempo. It took me back to a thousand bygone days, when we logged more than a million miles on a bus. The 45-foot mass of iron sped across the Southeastern states en route back to Nashville. I felt saddened that the special weekend had to end. I was always a homebody, the one who couldn't wait to get back to the house. Not that day. In Nashville, a somber meeting was ahead. The situation was out of my hands and I could not stop the inevitable.

There's an eerie calm before a storm. I had a sense of being in a pavilion, prepared by the Lord, and I was protected. The best part was that He was right there with me and He was not surprised.

For in the time of trouble he shall hide me in his pavilion: in the secret of his tabernacle shall he hide me: he shall set me upon a rock.

(Psalm 27:5 - KJV)

In the ensuing months, I rode an emotional roller-coaster, sinking to the bottom of a miry pit, and clawing my way back to the rock, fighting harder each time. Stormy rains were producing mud, while that very mud held precious seeds of promise. Those seeds would germinate and grow, in the soil of my heart, by the watering of God's Word. There is always purpose in the mud.

As the rain and the snow come down from heaven, and do not return to it without watering the earth and making it bud and flourish, so that it yields seed for the sower and bread for the eater, so is my word that goes out from my mouth; It will not return to me empty, but will accomplish what I desire and achieve the purpose for which I sent it.

(Isaiah 55:10 & 11 - NIV)

Cindy and I sat in the gynecologist's office at St. Thomas hospital. I had mixed emotions about meeting this renowned specialist—the doctor who took on "difficult cases." Cindy and I tried to take in the complicated medical jargon, but it was just another doctor, pointing to cryptic images from my MRI, lit up on a wall in yet another consultation office. Shaking his head, as if somewhat bewildered, the doctor said, "This is not an operable cancer, in my opinion. Your vital organs are too involved in the mass. There's nothing I can do to help you. I am a surgeon. You need an oncologist. Get aggressive with chemo and hope for the best. Dr. Anderson will get back with you and help you move forward." Any glimmer of hope I had for a new beginning was snuffed out.

For Cindy's sake, I put on a brave mask. I tried not to let my raw emotions loose. At the same time, my heartsick daughter was wearing her own mask. Slowly making our way through the afternoon traffic, we made a futile attempt to sort out what the doctor had said. Pounding away at my consciousness was a brutal awareness:

The doctors—all of them—consider me a hopeless case. They quickly pass me to the next one in line.

Part of me was somewhat relieved that surgery was not an option. If only that were the end of the story and I could go on with life. It seemed the more I learned, the less I knew.

I felt curiously invisible in the perpetual motion of life around me. People rushed around like mad, jostling for lane changes, honking for no apparent reason, and getting all worked up. Why? Like an alien, I looked on from a different dimension, no longer marching to the cadence of this planet. The beat of life had been interrupted and I was hopelessly out of step.

Ominous warnings rang in my ears, telling me that this storm was different. I knew that I must dig deeper than ever before and hold on for dear life. Strangely, I also had no doubt that I would survive. I drew on the strength of Florida's blessings... drinking from the living waters of promise.

God allows certain mud for certain seasons and certain reasons. That does not change the fact that the mud feels bad and seems endless.

The Texas storms that I so vividly recall, cleansed the dusty atmosphere. Torrents of rain descended from the big sky and instantly bathed everything beneath. Then, a fresh new day appeared. As a kid, I loved the residue of sandy mud around the yard. It provided the perfect environment for us kids to play. That mud, in little hands, turned into pies that baked in the vast oven of hot sunshine. Even then, I was learning to make something out of the mud.

Dr. Jordan Berlin, an oncologist, was the next physician to review my records. Levoy and I were surprised when he and three other doctors entered the room where we were waiting. Four different doctors presented their opinions. Each one stated his case for the particular method of treatment he represented, laying out in great detail the expected or possible outcome. Each approach had an upside and a downside; benefits versus the side effects. Every scenario was discussed that morning. Only one doctor was a proponent of surgery.

So, surgery was an option?

The others were aligned with the doctor at St. Thomas, contending that surgery was not a feasible consideration. For an hour I felt like a potato, tossed back and forth, too hot to handle. I could not begin to follow all the points of the varying opinions. I was starving for the tiniest morsel of encouragement. There was not one.

The doctors had difficulty putting their stamp of approval on a definite method of treatment. Given the unique challenges presented, such as the type of cancer and its involvement of other vital organs, they were appropriately cautious. The best course of action was not obvious. Although the doctors had differing opinions, each did his best. Nevertheless, I was weary from the struggle, and my mind rejected the extreme measures put before us. The doctors agreed that Levoy and I needed to talk to a plastic surgeon, who explained the procedure to remove muscle from my legs to rebuild tissues that would be taken out of the pelvic area. Plastic surgery would take place immediately after the cancerous tissue was removed. The doctor rarely lifted his eyes from the folder on his lap, as he described the proposed surgery in graphic detail. He stressed the fact that his part of the procedure was merely cosmetic, but not life-extending. Its purpose was designed to enhance a positive state of mind and sense of womanhood.

When the doctor finished, Levoy asked immediately, "Are you saying that you would take muscle from my wife's legs and completely remake parts of her body? Is that what you do when a man wants to become a woman?"

"You have the general idea, Mr. Dewey." The doctor continued writing. He still did not make eye contact with either of us.

Levoy stated emphatically, "If you're doing this for my benefit, you can forget it. My wife has suffered enough. There's nothing wrong with her legs and I don't want them cut."

Our clicking footsteps echoed in the hollow corridor as Levoy and I hurried toward the exit. As my husband of 40-plus years reached for my clammy hand, I felt an assuring squeeze. "Honey," Levoy said softly, "You've been my sweetheart for a long time. Nothing, absolutely nothing, will ever change that." The caring words of my devoted husband were a comforting balm to my bitter soul. We slipped sadly through the revolving door of the building into the vast unknown. Strange as it seems, I saw the hand of God that day.

When terminal illness threatens, one clings to words of hope, like someone lost at sea in a raging tempest, hanging onto a floatation ring for dear life.

Soon after hearing that cancer had returned, we had services at Victory Temple in Grand Prairie, Texas. Max Heflin, a dear brother, encouraged me with a special, prophetic word that God impressed upon his heart: "The cancer is encapsulated and will not spread." Max's words confirmed what God had already shown me through much prayer and study. The words lodged in my spirit and gave me strength throughout the long road ahead.

Our good friends, Roger and Barbara McDuff, told us about a clinic across the border where people receive unconventional treatments for cancer. They were personal friends of Dr. Francisco Contreras, who is the son of the founder of Oasis of Hope, a facility near Tijuana, Mexico. A pioneer of modern medicine, Dr. Earnesto Contreras is credited with coining the term, "Holistic Medicine."

Oasis of Hope is known for its success in treating cancer by using alternative methods, occasionally combined with modern medicine. Levoy and I did some research and were impressed with the amazing record of patients who found their path to healing in this obscure place. Waiting for the doctors at Vanderbilt Hospital to make a decision was disheartening, and we were grasping for answers. The holistic approach was becoming increasingly attractive. After four months, with no definite course of action on the traditional medical side, the strain had taken a toll on the entire family.

The option of going to Mexico was intriguing. Only finances stood in our way. Once my husband prays through about something, nothing stands in his way. He never mentioned the sacrifice he had made, but I knew. Our dreams were on hold and our plans had already been set aside. Fighting this battle took everything. My heart was profoundly touched to see how Levoy was so willing to walk away from it all. He explained, "I'll do anything in my power to get you well. We'll start over and God will help us."

Word spread across the country that thousands of dollars were needed. Our network of friends went into action and the telephone started ringing off the hook. Those who responded to this need shall ever be endeared to us. My heart warmed at the generosity of people who willingly became involved. I didn't know we had so many friends. In a few weeks we were in a position to make arrangements with Oasis of Hope.

For the first time since the diagnosis of recurring colorectal cancer, someone offered hope. It had been 16 months since Dr. Anderson gave us the bad news. The road had been rough and windy, but now, highlighted on our calendar were 21 days in April 2003. Medical records were submitted, correspondence was exchanged and preadmission was completed. Levoy and I would soon be on our way to Mexico.

Hope is a beautiful thing.

Our flight landed in San Diego, where we spent the night, although anxiety prevented sleep. The next morning a van took us from the Holiday Inn to Tijuana. That afternoon we arrived at the Oasis of Hope, quietly situated in the little Mexican border town. Guest accommodations and the treatment facility were contained within a two-story hospital. The second floor was arranged to house patients who were not hospitalized. The ground floor of the facility was reserved for bedridden individuals. We checked into the modest room reserved for us. It was immaculately clean, freshly painted in hues of soft pink, with two twin beds, and a television. We felt at home right away and very comfortable with the cordial people in charge of the operation. Oasis of Hope had a vibrant atmosphere with an upbeat, Christian environment.

A sunny afternoon welcomed us to Mexico and the salty ocean breeze of the Pacific gently called. We could hardly wait to take a five-minute stroll to the beach. The warm sand worked its magic on our weary, bare feet, as we walked slowly along the water's edge. Our footprints in the sand were quickly washed away by the white capped waves that lapped onto the shore. The deep blue ocean stretched as far as the eye could see and touched the backdrop of a blazing orange sunset. The sight was breathtaking. We were awed as we gazed upon the magnitude and artistry of God's creation. The Creator wants His children to find pleasure in His handiwork, and we did. In that short respite, we lost track of time and were refreshed in the lap of His wonder.

The all wise God walks upon the face of the deep that He spoke into existence, yet He leaves no footprints. Who can know the mystery of His ways? Oh no! Cancer was not a problem for such a God.

> **By the word of the Lord the heavens were made and all the host of them by the breath of His mouth; He gathers the waters of the sea together as a heap; He lays up the deep in storehouses.**
> (Psalm 33:6-7 - NKJV)

Dusk was falling fast. Levoy and I lingered on the beach for as long as possible. We promised one another that we would return to that peaceful beach every day. Quietly, we made our way back to the hospital, hand in hand.

Tomorrow would be a big day.

My initial meeting with the doctors was encouraging. Hope permeated the atmosphere and that was healing in itself. Prayer was encouraged and considered a vital part of regaining health and wellness. I was assigned to Dr. Gene Dessourde, who would supervise my treatments and chart my progress. He wrote my daily regimen—my schedule for the next three weeks—in meticulous detail.

The first job was to begin the detoxification process, which was the purpose for the special diet. The objective was to rid the body of toxins—poisons—and achieve an alkaline pH balance. Studies show that consuming acid-producing foods results in toxins which are believed to be a contributing factor in cancer. Many additives, chemicals and other substances in foods (especially processed foods) are proven carcinogens. It turns out that just about everything we touch, breathe, and eat affects our health. When more toxins are introduced into the system than the body can throw off, the cells are compromised. The regimen of physical detoxification must become a habit, because of the constant contamination from carcinogens to which we are subjected.

Breakfast was a preview of what was to be offered in the dining room. Patients were not allowed to have coffee, tea, salt, butter, dairy products, meat, sugar, bread or pastries. Green leafy vegetables were juiced and it was mandatory that patients drink two large glasses of this vitamin-rich beverage every day. A diet of organic fruits and vegetables was the mainstay for all participants of the program. The process of purging was excruciating. I will never forget that first week—the severe headaches and flu-like symptoms. My body adjusted slowly to the new diet.

The Apostle Paul speaks of the daily renewing of the mind; a kind of "spiritual detoxification." The Word of God is a "detox" for the soul. Spiritual cleansing is wrenching to the flesh, yet necessary to achieve a life of overcoming. Disease within the spirit starts with a small, seemingly harmless discrepancy or compromise that grows into the malignancy of sin. Something as harmless as a negative thought or secret activity will invade the spirit, if it is not stopped. The demise is a long process, rather than a one-time event.

> *...do not be conformed to this world, but be transformed by the renewing of your mind, that you may prove what is that good and acceptable and perfect will of God.* (Romans 12:2 - NKJV)

Have you ever seen the rhythmic "blips," known as QRS complexes, on a hospital monitor as you sat beside a friend or loved one? When the heart stops beating, the monitor shows a straight line; this is known as "flat-lining."

On the second day at Oasis of Hope, I underwent a simple surgical procedure to implant a portable catheter—a "port-a-cath"—through which I would receive all medications. When mysterious complications developed, I "flatlined" on the operating table.

The unthinkable stopping of my heart could have caused my death. Thankfully, I was successfully resuscitated. As I struggled to wake up, still lying on the table, I heard Dr. Dessourde shouting at a nurse in Spanish. I didn't know exactly what was being said, but I sensed something bad had happened. The interpretation of the doctor's words came a bit later:

"Oh, my God," Dr Dessourde yelled, "Get another doctor in here! Now! Hurry! This woman is dying!" He shouted the words over and over. Then he yelled at me in English, "Come on...come on...come on, lady! You cannot do this! You are not going to die on me!"

When I finally opened my eyes, people were rushing around my bed. There was a state of controlled panic. The doctor said I could have died that day. No one knew exactly why this quirky incident happened during a routine procedure. The irony was that cancer was threatening my life, yet the routine implantation of a port-a-cath could have ended it abruptly.

I made history at Oasis of Hope and, believe me, there was absolutely no pleasure in the recognition. Almost every time I saw Dr. Dessourde after the incident, he shook his head from side to side and said, "Lady, you scared me...BAD!"

Levoy's willingness to comply with rules of the organic diet at Oasis of Hope was a bit of a surprise. He managed very well with the food offered in the cafeteria, and he was a trooper in honoring the guidelines. Once a week, patients' companions were taken to a restaurant in Tijuana, where steak was on the menu, and he looked forward to the change of diet.

Some very happy patients were at Oasis of Hope for their follow-up appointments. Others, like me, were there for the first time. Interacting with people from all over the world, who had found this place of healing, was inspiring. A lady from Great Britain had been coming every six months for the past two years, continuing her treatments and evaluation. She was in remission. On the strength of her excellent reports and recommendation, many additional cancer patients had made the long journey from the U.K. to Oasis of Hope.

There was an emaciated young Italian man in a wheelchair, whose condition had been dismissed as untreatable by doctors in Europe. His sister and brother-in-law accompanied him to Oasis of Hope. I could not understand their conversation, but the anxiety of their hearts needed no interpretation.

Mary, from Illinois, was trying so hard to live for her grandchildren and her husband. They had been married only a few short months when she was stricken with breast cancer. By the time it was diagnosed, the cancer had spread to her lungs and bones. She was a devout Catholic and we prayed together every afternoon in the dining room. Soon after I returned home, word came that she had lost her hard fight.

One gentleman returned for three days of reevaluation, tests and more medication. He was from San Angelo, Texas, where Levoy's brother is a pastor. Although the man's body was diseased and weak, his faith was strong. He proudly showed pictures of his lovely wife and three small children. We exchanged addresses. I hoped we could visit him on one of our trips out west. How saddened I was to hear that he passed from this life a short time after our meeting.

Church services were held in the main dining room every Sunday morning. A local minister arranged the order of services and preached the Gospel of Jesus Christ. It was a refreshing time of praise and worship.

Levoy and I were invited to provide the music and share about our journey of previously surviving cancer. I was scheduled for intravenous medications every Sunday and I'm sure I must have looked odd, playing an electric keyboard for the worship service while hooked up to the I.V. drip.

The services were opportunities for patients to encourage one another. The story in *John 9* was very appropriate. I told the cancer patients at Oasis of Hope about the blind man who found healing in an unconventional way. It was easy for all of us to identify with his journey to the pool. We were at an oasis and, at the same time, caught in the midst of a lot of mud.

Faith comes by hearing and hearing by the Word of God. Reaching out to others strengthens faith in the healing power of Jesus. That is good incentive to accept invitations to share what God has done for me. I truly believe that our steps were—and are—ordered by the Lord. I also believe that part of my purpose in going to Mexico was fulfilled on those Sunday mornings, as I shared my personal story.

The unconventional methods for fighting cancer at the Oasis of Hope were determined on an individual basis. It was decided that the best treatments for me were chelation, oxygenation and laetrile. Chamomile tea and coffee enemas, in conjunction with the special diet, were also part of my daily routine.

When I told Cindy and Susie about the enemas, I expected their witty responses. Sure enough, some very funny remarks were passed among friends and family. They wanted to know if I took my coffee and tea enemas with cream and sugar. I assured them that those condiments were contraband at Oasis of Hope. Since then, "tea-time" and "coffee-break" have taken on new meanings.

Most of the patients were connected to I.V.'s during the day. All around the facility, we pulled clear vinyl bags of medicine, hanging from I.V. poles. Most patients became very queasy while undergoing the treatments. We were assured by the medical staff that our bodies were responding in a positive way and that the side effects would subside. Procedures that detoxify the body of heavy metals and other impurities were constantly discussed and taught. Group classes were mandatory and very helpful.

A specific test for a tumor marker—called carcinoembryonic antigen (CEA)—was performed when I arrived at Oasis of Hope, and was repeated periodically throughout my stay. Tumor markers often appear in the tissues or blood of cancer patients. They are produced either by the cancer itself or, more likely, by one's own tissues in response to the cancer. Alone, they are inadequate to make a diagnosis of cancer, but they are useful in following patients for cancer recurrence. CEA was elevated in my case, as it had been when I was initially diagnosed with colorectal cancer almost nine years earlier.

I was aware of the uphill battle, facing a terminal illness that had returned after such a long period of time. The cancer was categorized as inoperable by the doctors at Oasis of Hope and, after three weeks, the tumor marker indicated that cancer was still present. More disappointment—more mud—accumulated.

A critical decision for continuing treatments was discussed. The recommendation by the Oasis of Hope Tumor Board was chemotherapy, the last option in their regimen. Chemotherapy was reserved for extremely rare cases and only when all other measures had been exhausted. Hearing those words was a major emotional setback; it was the low point of my stay in Mexico.

The drug they recommended was 5FU, the same drug used to treat my first colon cancer. Although it was effective before, Levoy and I suspected it was no longer cutting-edge. I wanted the latest and most effective treatment available. In the United States, I would have the most current chemotherapy, along with the advantage of insurance coverage. We decided to return home.

In a final meeting with the doctors at Oasis of Hope, I agreed to finish the laetrile injections at home. The port-a-cath on my chest would remain in place for that purpose. I attended additional classes to learn the rigors of self-medication, and the doctors wrote a detailed schedule to follow. Before leaving, I obtained enough medication to complete the month-long regimen. I braced myself for the side effects and sickness I had already experienced, and made the commitment to give it my very best effort, regardless of the discomfort.

We climbed aboard the van that waited alongside the hospital to take us across the border. Six other patients also headed home that day. The grace of God sustained me like a rock. I functioned by His strength and an optimistic steadiness of spirit, even though I had not gotten the desired results. The hot Mexican sun shined down on the little group as we made our departure. God was surely smiling on His needy children in that vehicle. Spirits were bright, reflecting the day God gifted. Like a needle sliding through cloth, the driver skillfully maneuvered the vehicle through the crowded streets of Tijuana.

Along the bumpy road, compelling stories were exchanged. Our backgrounds and lives were diverse, but our hearts were united with a common desire to live, free of cancer. Some had glowing reports of amazing changes in their bodies. Others, like me, would seek different paths to wellness.

There were no negative words or regrets from the passengers in our bus. Everyone agreed that the holistic treatments at Oasis of Hope had been a positive experience. Although every battle was not won, we had received help in our personal wars and pledged to fight on.

I was physically exhausted when we returned home from Mexico. Continuing the injections was difficult, as uncontrollable chills shook my body for two hours after each treatment. At the time, Suzanne, Nathan and their young boys occupied the apartment in our house. Their proximity was a timely blessing, because they were available around the clock to support and help us in many ways. The little boys were a diversion and rays of much needed sunshine. When the grandchildren were present, I guarded my words from the tender ears that were ever open. I was saddened that cancer occupied the lives of my family; it was on everyone's mind and it worked its way into every conversation.

I was glad when the school bus came and 10 year-old Elijah could escape the ordeal around the house. His keen sensitivity was unusual and he felt the impact of my health issues. He would often slip into the bedroom to check on me when I was having a chill. He would quietly lie face down on top of the layers of blankets that were piled on me. The weight of his body was comforting and his breath warmed me. God's presence is most precious when it manifests in the love of a child. I was gently reminded of the reasons I was fighting so hard. When my teeth stopped chattering, Elijah slipped away to do the things that little boys normally do. I knew that his concern represented all my little ones, praying for their Mimi. Kids go through mud, too.

My grandson reminded me of the Prophet Elijah. The Bible says that he placed his own body upon a dead baby and breathed life into it. He refused to accept death. God answered his plea and restored the child to life. This time, I was the baby.

P R A **Y** E R

YIELD!

He comes by invitation only.

"Into my heart, into my heart; Come into my heart, Lord Jesus; Come in today, Come in to stay, Come into my heart, Lord Jesus..." You probably sang this little song when you were a child, too.

When Jesus came the first time there was no room for Him in the inn. The Christ child was cradled in a lowly manger with the animals, but Mary and Joseph knew their baby boy was the Savior. The wise men found Him. Wise men *still* find Him and worship Him. Calendars will ever reflect the advent of Jesus' remarkable birth. His coming changed the world. He still changes the hearts of those who bid Him come.

The wisest thing you will ever do is make room for Jesus. He knows all about the things that took place yesterday. He knows what's happening today. He even knows what is coming your way tomorrow. Jesus loves you and He's waiting to be invited into your world...and make it better.

You will show me the path of life; In Your presence is fullness of joy; At Your right hand are pleasures forevermore. (Psalm 16:11 - NKJV)

PRAYER: *I don't know what I would do without You, dear Jesus. Your presence is so real to me. I have been chosen to bear special scars and I don't feel worthy. Give me the grace to face each challenge one step at a time. Thank You for placing within my heart a desire to bring glory to Your name and make a difference in this hurting world.* Amen.

5

Envision the Victory

*L*imbo is not a desirable place. Like the blind man, I encountered the Lord and was on my way to the pool, but there was an awful lot of mud. Things were certainly not working out like I had planned. I had already been tossed back and forth by more doctors than I dared count. The tumor was growing steadily. No surgeon wanted to touch it. The prognosis had not changed, just rephrased. The doctors in Mexico agreed that the cancer was inoperable. There were still no answers.

God's grace sustained me and was all-sufficient. I had no clue what the pool would look like or how the victory would come, but I knew that His steadfast Word would not fail. By faith, I kept moving. I absolutely refused to give up.

People called from across the United States and beyond, wanting the latest report. I was too weak to talk on the phone, so the news was relayed by others. It was a big challenge for my daughters and Levoy to repeat the details and to speak their faith at the same time. Without faith, none of it made sense.

At the same time there was another trauma developing. Some say trouble comes in pairs. Cancer was not the only storm raging. We were also treading the devastating waters of bankruptcy. Several factors contributed to filing Chapter 11. Mother's health was declining and I needed to be at home with her. My ability to travel was limited and that put a strain on our income. When I had cancer the first time, Levoy continued traveling without me. Now things were different. Booking services was hard and he was near exhaustion. Our backs were against the wall. My husband has always been resourceful. Ever since we started traveling, raising funds to support the ministry was often a necessity. In order to make ends meet, we had three business interests that supplemented our finances. When all three businesses went under at approximately the same time, recovering from the losses was impossible. Circumstances we could not control snowballed and thousands of dollars owed to us could not be recouped.

Our personal tragedies peaked on September 11, 2001. The collapsing towers in New York City were a visual parallel to what we were experiencing at home. It felt like terrorists were attacking the foundation of our existence.

In the end, we lost two properties, our excellent credit rating, and a lot of foolish pride. Fortunately that is not the end of the story. What we gained was even more significant, and eternal: a new trust in God, more empathy for others, knowledge, and the will to start over again. In the end, we gained far more than we lost.

The victories were manifested in our faith in God that had grown stronger through the hardship. No institution, no man and no circumstance could steal the treasures embedded within our hearts. Our spirits were not bankrupt. We were richly blessed and thriving.

Before we married, Levoy and I attended Southwestern Bible Institute, a small Bible School near Dallas, Texas. Today it has grown to be a respectable university and is situated on an impressive campus in Waxahachie. Many of the relationships we made in those days endure today. The discerning hearts of longtime friends were burdened for my healing and our overall well-being. Their prayers during the toughest time of our lives have endeared them to us for all time. Our Alma Mater wanted to help in a practical way, by having a fund-raiser in our honor. Levoy and I were hesitant at first, because we did not relish the thought of revealing our needs publicly. Finally, we agreed to bring our family to Waxahachie for an "Appreciation

Concert." The date was set and arrangements made for the event to take place at Evangel Temple.

Ronnie Shortes, Levoy's best man in our wedding, was instrumental in taking care of details at the local level. Ronnie and his wife, Sylvia, had been loyal friends and strong supporters of our ministry for many years. Ronnie secured the church and his pastor, Rev. John Bates, participated in the service.

Ruth Finley, a dear friend and minister from Lonoke, Arkansas, was the coordinator of promotions. She notified the school's "Ole Frenz" alumni network, and painstakingly spread the word via email and mail-outs.

About a month prior to the concert, Nathan approached me with a small request. He said, "Poppy needs a new song for this event. When we decide on the song, I'll get him in the studio and record it."

I agreed that it was a very good idea. So I asked, "Do you have a particular one in mind?" I hoped that he would have already decided on the perfect song.

To my chagrin, he answered, "Suzanne wrote a chorus...thought you might write some verses."

I protested. "Nathan, I haven't written in months. I don't feel like it. Honestly, I'm dry...dry as a shuck...no creative juices flowing. By the way, when do you need the lyrics?"

Calm as a cucumber he continued, "Don't worry, I'm in no hurry. Tomorrow afternoon will be soon enough."

"Tomorrow afternoon? Get real!" I exclaimed.

Nathan walked out of the room without another word. He knew I would be thinking about that song. Sure enough, I couldn't get the catchy little chorus off my mind: *"I know there's victory for me...I know there's victory for me...I fasted and I prayed...then God made a way...da, da, da."*

I found myself at the computer pounding the keyboard with a fury. The fatigue from fighting a deadly disease momentarily washed away. The words poured into my spirit like a fountain and spilled over the keyboard and onto the screen in front of my eyes. Never had lyrics flowed so freely. A writer knows when the anointing is present and when it is not. I discovered, long ago, I can write nothing of significance without the Lord. That day, the scales fell off my weeping eyes and I could mentally picture a time when I would be cancer-free. I envisioned the miracle!

Later that evening, I picked up the phone and called my son-in-law, who had asked the impossible only hours before. I simply said, "I'm ready for you to check out this song. The lyrics are done. I think you'll like them."

Nathan wasn't at all surprised. He knew that I work best under pressure. He wrote an amazing arrangement, added a bridge and produced the song. *Victory for Me* was the title of Levoy's new CD. It was introduced, right on time, to our friends in Waxahachie.

Victory for Me

Words by Suzanne Young & Cleon Dewey
Music & Bridge by Nathan Young

Chorus
I know there is victory for me
I know there is victory for me,
I fasted and I prayed
Then God made a way
I know there is victory for me.

1
Every cherished dream
is now surrendered to His will
I'm trusting in the One who cannot fail
Anticipation stirs within my waiting soul
He's Lord of my tomorrows –
I will come forth as pure gold.

2
Emotions like an army invade a doubting mind
But the Word of God prevails against the foe

Suddenly the essence of hope fills the air
In the ruins of disappointment –
I behold my Lord is standing there.

3
No weapon formed against me shall ever prosper
Nothing can separate me from His love
My heart hungers for a happy jubilee
So I will sing and I will dance –
And He will set my spirit free.

Bridge
Through the rain – Through the pain –
Through my fear
Through my tears – I know there's victory for me
Stand through your rain – Through your pain
Through your fears – Through your tears
I know – I know there's victory for me.

Once again, our son-in-law, Mark, secured a Prevost bus for the Texas trip. We so appreciated the kind gesture from the Hemphill Brother's Coach Company, where Mark is Vice-President. The grandchildren were excused from school and their parents made the necessary adjustments in work schedules. Everything was set for the trip, and Levoy and I were delighted to have everyone together for another concert.

It was a great reunion with family and friends, and an unforgettable evening of music and ministry.

Levoy, Cindy, Suzanne and Nathan sang the glory down that night. It was marvelous! Mark played the bass guitar and helped run the sound board. *Victory for Me* was powerfully anointed and I felt humbled to have had a part in writing the lyrics.

Most importantly, corporate prayers ascended to the Father on our behalf. Levoy was in his own private world of pain. My dear husband's anguish could not be medicated. He had always been the one who fixed broken things, but not this time.

I concluded the event with a few personal thoughts. One more time, God stretched me far beyond my own will and abilities. I spoke to the audience in Waxahachie about the mud of *John 9*. It was an opportune moment for me to reflect. Surviving a previous terminal illness was cause for being thankful. When cancer returned, the blind man's story had a profound effect on my faith once again, and my resolve to fight was renewed as I spoke about it. The declaration of my faith, combined with the prayers in that room, was a line drawn in the sand. God answered prayer and my health was miraculously restored in 1994, after the doctor had given me three months to live. Our family and friends were gathered in one accord to beseech the Lord for another miracle.

We stood around the altar at the close of the concert. Hands were raised as praises ascended to the Throne of God for His mighty works and the victories yet to manifest. The song, *Victory for Me*, played on the public address system as we prayed for one another. Our family's faith was bolstered, just to know that our loving friends would continue believing and praying until the answer came.

> **Assuredly, I say to you, whatever you bind on earth will be bound in Heaven, and whatever you loose on earth will be loosed in Heaven. Again I say to you that if two of you agree on earth concerning anything that they ask, it will be done for them by My Father in heaven. For where two or three are gathered together in My name, I am there in the midst of them.** (Matthew 18:18-20 - NKJV)

Something remarkable happened during that time of prayer. Pastor Bates walked across the front area of the auditorium toward me. His countenance revealed that he had something to say. This is what I heard: "You will have twelve more years of ministry. You will live beyond that time, but you will have twelve more years of fruitful ministry."

Those words, from the pastor of Evangel Temple, kept my vision clear through many dark nights. I never forgot them. Many times it appeared impossible, in the natural sense, that I would ever return to the ministry or even live through the illness. At those times, I turned my thoughts to that night in Waxahachie, Texas.

A large group met for breakfast the next morning. The restaurant pulsed with the roar of laughter and the sounds of folks having a good time together. Funny stories and quite a few pranks from schooldays were told for the umpteenth time. We mused about the misdemeanors and feats of our youth that had grown bigger, better, and even exaggerated into the believe-it-or-not category, with every passing year. Necks were hugged and promises were spoken to keep in touch. As a family, we expressed our deep gratitude for the generous support of those extraordinary people. The Dewey clan settled in the bus for the return trip to Nashville. Our hearts were full as we departed Waxahachie with such rich memories.

Things change when people pray for others. It happened to me that night in Waxahachie. God's presence, which descended on the concert, lingered in my soul. The concerns that weighed me down, about not living long enough to fulfill my purpose, were gone. My destiny was envisioned afresh. I simply believed it, received it and started acting like I was going to live.

In those days Hezekiah was sick and near death. And Isaiah the prophet, the son of Amoz, went to him and said to him, "Thus says the Lord: Set your house in order, for you shall die, and not live." Then he turned his face toward the wall, and prayed to the Lord, saying, "Remember now, O

Lord, I pray, how I have walked before You in truth and with a loyal heart, and have done what was good in Your sight." And Hezekiah wept bitterly. And it happened, before Isaiah had gone out into the middle court, that the word of the Lord came to him, saying, "Return and tell Hezekiah the leader of my people, Thus says the Lord, the God of David your father: I have heard your prayer, I have seen your tears; surely I will heal you. On the third day you shall go up to the house of the Lord. And I will add to your days fifteen years. I will deliver you and this city from the hand of the king of Assyria; and I will defend this city for my own sake, and for the sake of my servant David."

(II Kings 20:1-6 - NKVJ)

This account of King Hezekiah encouraged my heart. He was told by the Prophet Isaiah to set his house in order, because he was going to die. God heard Hezekiah's supplication and granted him an additional fifteen years.

God added years to his life. Why not mine?

When I was 14, I had an experience that was traumatic, though not life threatening, and even a little funny. The story is a metaphor of literal mud and spiritual mud.

It was summer and my family was in South Dakota. Even now, I conjure mental images of long, sultry days; dusty harvest fields; sitting on prickly wheat stubble and eating in the shade of the truck; augers tumbling golden grain into bins and dump trucks; driving too soon; kids doing men's work; playing crazy pranks; being covered in dirt from head to toe; physical exhaustion; and the incomparable satisfaction of hard work.

The section of land was barren of grain and it looked as if a giant razor had given it a crew-cut. There was an immense sense of relief when the crop was safely secure and in the elevator. It was time to move to the next field of ripened grain. We had to move all of the equipment about five miles, around several sections of land; too short a distance to load the combine onto a truck.

Daddy had given me explicit orders to follow closely behind the big machine in the car. I was driving my brother's 1939 Studebaker.

The John Deere combine ran at the break-neck speed of about 10 miles per hour. It was a boring task and almost impossible for me to be disciplined enough to drive so slowly. I was just learning to drive and wanted to go faster. There were a couple of combines, two or three dump trucks, a pickup that Mother was driving, and the old Studebaker. I was tired of following behind everyone else in the caravan and eating their dust!

Granddad's fields were familiar to me. Woops! Daddy missed turning the green machine into the field at the flat spot in the ditch where we always turned. Why did he rumble past the shortcut across the field?

Without thinking, I made an impulsive sharp turn and headed across an unplowed corner of the field that was overgrown with tall grass. The foliage made a clicking sound on the bottom of the low riding car. It was music to my ears. I was giddy with the cadence of my error. Clickety-click, clickety-click...I was finally going fast. Thoughts of being the first one to the field, ahead of all the others, made me laugh out loud. A little sibling rivalry was always in play between my brother and me. Oh boy! I'd have a good one on him.

My euphoria vanished like a vapor in the hot Dakota wind. The old gray car suddenly started bogging down. Then it came to a dead stop. Oh no! I was in big trouble. I understood, much too late, why Daddy avoided the shortcut. The recent rains had resulted in a deep layer of mud, not visible underneath the tall grass. Daddy had remembered the recent rain; he knew there would be deep mud in that low grassy spot, and he also knew the certainty of getting stuck.

When the sight of my car, heading in the wrong direction, came into Daddy's peripheral vision, he saw what was coming next. The mud did not take him by surprise. His unsuspecting, impulsive daughter was about to be in big trouble. She would need his help. He stopped the procession of vehicles, jumped into the pickup truck and made a bee-line for the barn. He grabbed his high-topped rubber boots, climbed onto Granddad Nixon's big tractor, and headed for the damsel in distress. Daddy knew what to do.

Half an hour seemed like an eternity. I had a lot of time to think about the inconvenience I caused by my hasty decision. I felt forsaken in the mire. I got exactly what I deserved.

The big old tractor, chugging through the mud, came to the rescue. What a welcome sight! Fortunately, Daddy had a good sense of humor. My hide was saved many a time by his ability to see the funny side of things. He hopped off the high seat of the tractor with a grin on his well-tanned face. His usual question already coming out his mouth, "Well, what did you learn from this deal?"

For some unexplainable reason, I stepped out of the car and stood in mud up to my knees, bawling and squalling like a baby calf in a hail storm. Indeed, I needed somebody's help; somebody bigger and wiser than me. "Daddy," I cried, "I'm sorry. Okay, I learned to follow your orders better. Next time I'll stay close behind you."

You can believe I prayed that day in the old car, stuck in the mud. The Father foresaw our frailties long ago and He made a way of escape, through Jesus. He sees our folly and meets us at our point of need. Some problems are self-induced like my driving headlong into the mud, while other difficulties have little to do with choices. Whatever the case, God shows up with the answer. He turns circumstances around. All we have to do is call upon Him. The Father is never surprised and He always knows what to do.

Jesus set the example of how to pray. Prayer is always in order. No one has ever been condemned for having too much faith or praying too much. Every petition should be prefaced with the Lord's Prayer: *"Thy will be done on earth as it is in Heaven."* On the cross, Jesus surrendered to the will of his Heavenly Father. Every battle waged against the human race was won on Calvary's cross by Christ's divine obedience.

Everyone is in some kind of mud. We all have issues. Take courage! There is help in time of need. God heals in different ways and by various means.

When Jesus spat on the ground, made mud and smeared it on the blind man's eyes, He showed that the Healer can use what He wills. It just might be chemo, radiation, surgery, holistic medicine, something else, or nothing at all. Whether medicinal properties were present in the mud that Jesus made, we do not know. We do know that Jesus is still the Healer of broken bodies, hearts and lives.

Hope long deferred makes the heart sick...
(Proverbs 13·12 - KJV)

Although there were times when I didn't know where I was or what to do, giving up was not an option. Faith would not be necessary if this were a perfect world. Even though I grew tired of the process I was undergoing, my eyes refused to see anything less than a victorious conclusion.

Our family went to a church in Wanchese, North Carolina every year. It was one of our favorite places to visit because of its colorful people and picturesque location near the Atlantic Ocean. This quaint coastal village on the outer banks is located near Kitty Hawk, where the Wright brothers made their first successful flight. The surrounding area is rich in history and we loved it. Most of the local people were sustained by commercial fishing. Some owned their own boats. We also enjoyed the succulent bounty of the sea at the church dinners. Maybe that was why we returned year after year. The flounder was absolutely delicious!

The girls were amused by some of the people who came to church barefooted. Since I enjoy taking off my shoes at the piano, I fit right in with that group.

One afternoon Levoy had an interesting conversation with an old, seasoned fisherman, who had just dropped off his burlap bag, full of oysters, by the kitchen. He helped us carry some of our equipment into the building. There was a dark bank of clouds building on the horizon, which led to the subject of the weather. The old gentleman started telling tales of surviving the storms at sea.

In his thick brogue, he shared his experience exuberantly, "When you be stuck in a stome at sea, you neva wanna try ta out run ah. Da winds...day roll you ova and you go unda. What you do, my Brodda, you turn da bow ah da ship right into da teeth ah da stome. You not eva gonna drop da anchah in da stome. Dat pop da front right outa da boat. You bedda push da throttle wide open...hold ah tight...and ride ah out."

The way the old fisherman spoke about the storms was not forgotten as I navigated through the mud of cancer. The same principle works in any storm. I did not run away, in panic and fear, from the storm of cancer. That would have meant turning my back on God. Instead, I turned the bow of my boat into the teeth of the storm and rode it out.

Life threatening issues will make one stop and look at things in a different light. Some of my past impulsive actions, like this one, kept my spirits high:

Our first bus had lots of mechanical problems. Some good friends, the Palser's of Scots Bluff, Nebraska, owned a Harley Davidson shop. They saw our plight and gifted us with a small motorcycle. In the event of a breakdown, one of the guys could jump on the Harley and go for help. Cell phones were uncommon then. We must have been an amusing sight with that thing affixed to the front of the old green, GM bus.

Just about everyone in the group had taken their turn riding the new toy, except me. Although I had never ridden a motorcycle, it looked easy enough. After all it was a little thing. I announced, "My turn is next."

Levoy was less than enthusiastic. He questioned, "Do you know how to stop it?"

That insulted me. I assured my cautious husband, "I know all about it. I've been driving a car since I could crawl."

We were parked at a country church, somewhere in Ohio. It had been raining and the ground was very muddy. I wasn't concerned. I threw my leg over the bike, situated my confident self on the seat, and cranked the handle-bars so I could hear the engine roar. Away I went, like a wild bull out of the shoot. I was doing just fine; that is, until I saw that I was headed straight for a thicket of trees.

Oops! Maybe I should have checked out those brakes before I took off.

I looked to the right. There was a ditch. Impulsively, I cut to the left and took a safe landing in a huge mud puddle. Mud never looked so good, even though I was lying in it and the bike was almost buried. The mud saved my reckless hide.

A lot of soap and water removed all traces of the mud that covered me from head to toe. My bruised ego was not so easily corrected. That was my first and last ride on a motorcycle. In a moment, I learned the danger of impulsive action and gained the wisdom to learn how to use the "brakes" in every situation.

When the injections from Mexico were finished, it was time to find an oncologist. I had promised my primary care physician that I would schedule a follow-up visit, and Dr. Anderson appeared to be relieved when I was finally prepared to submit to conventional methods. This competent doctor, who had cared for our entire family, had a barrage of questions about the "cockamamie" approach to cancer I encountered in Mexico. I answered his questions to the best of my ability, fully understanding his cause for concern. Dr. Anderson emphasized the fact that I was cornered in a messy situation with a fast-growing tumor.

It was decided that Dr. David Spigel, at Sarah Cannon Research Center, would be my oncologist. The late, great comedienne of Grand Ole Opry fame, Minnie Pearl, helped fund this cancer research center, which bears her off-stage name. From the moment I met doctor Spigel, I knew he was a godsend. He was not critical of my pursuing unconventional medicine out of the country. He was sincerely interested in hearing about my experience in Mexico.

I took the liberty of telling him, up front, "We are people of faith and we believe in miracles." Levoy and I were slightly caught off guard by his thoughtful reply, "My dad was an oncologist, as well. I've seen a lot of sickness in my time. That one word you said...well, it's not in my vocabulary. My objective is to extend your life and give you better quality of what is left, if possible."

The tumor in my abdomen had grown from the size of a plum to the size of a football since leaving Mexico. The doctors at Sarah Cannon agreed that surgery and chemotherapy were needed immediately. It was good to know that the doctors were of one mind; their solidarity was important to assure me that I was on the right path.

Tests confirmed there were no signs of cancer in my liver or any other organs. There had been a spot on my liver when I arrived in Mexico. At the end of the three week regimen, the spot was no longer visible. That was extremely welcome news. I will always believe that my treatments at Oasis of Hope arrested the spread of the disease, even though the primary tumor was still growing.

The Surgeon, William Polk, and the Urologist, Raoul Concepcion, worked with Dr. Spigel. The three doctors conferred with the Tumor Board at Sarah Cannon for a couple of weeks. More tests were ordered during that time and my lab results were closely monitored.

Levoy and I sat quietly in Dr. Polk's office. We stared at the black and white images on the viewing panel. He pointed to the abnormalities, explaining the precarious position of the invasive tumor. He reiterated the fact that the tumor was large and not contained within the colon, which completely changed the kind of procedure recommended. It was attached to the outer wall of the bladder. This indicated that the bladder must be excised, along with the tumor.

My heart literally ached as I looked at the travesty inside my body. The pictures were telling and undeniable. The findings were devastating. We listened to the details that Dr. Polk translated into laymen's terms. It was an uncanny replay of nine years before; different doctor; different office; same death sentence.

We met with Dr. Polk on several occasions. The prognosis was grim. His manner of communicating was blunt. The surgery was defined as a radical "pelvic exenteration." It was a rare surgery, but the only option left. He explained the procedure which involved removing all the pelvic organs and surrounding structures, including the perineum.

"This is a surgery no doctor ever wants to do," Dr. Polk said. "Too bad, but there's no other way to get that devil out of there. Only three to five patients in 1,000 survive the surgery." His statement carried a hard blow. It was difficult to imagine. The doctor was patient, understanding our apparent difficulty in grasping the magnitude of the mortality numbers that were repeated at every appointment. Perhaps he thought I would "chicken out" if I knew the odds.

Why would a sane woman submit to a procedure with such high risks? I saw the cancer in a different light; I saw it as mud. I was about to take the hardest step en route to the pool. God had given peace before, when my back was against the wall. When everything in my world was shifting, the Word of God remained steady. The promise of *Psalm 119:116* and the miracle of the mud in *John 9* were stamped upon my heart and clearly imprinted in my vision. I must not—no, I *would* not—allow things along the way to sabotage my faith.

Surgery was not what I wanted, but I had surrendered my will. At times, the mud was not easily defined, but I had learned that it comes in many forms. Above all else, there was that underlying assurance that God could not fail. I heard all of the bad reports as they came, one by one. They were merely medical numbers, not divine prophecies. What one believes, one makes happen. I was constantly guarded against the indictment of negativity.

My doctors were competent and knew all about medicine. What they did not know was my future. I had lived with a massive, fast moving tumor inside my abdomen for a very long time and the time had come to submit to radical surgery. Imagining what life would be like after the fact was impossible. My heart and mind were set, like flint, on living, not dying. I envisioned victory!

"For I know the plans I have for you," declares
the Lord, *"Plans to prosper you and not to harm
you, plans to give you hope and a future."*
(Jeremiah 29:11 - NIV)

A somber mood permeated the atmosphere the day we informed our children of the plans for surgery. Suzanne held me and sobbed until she had no more tears. She was constantly by my side at home, her sensitive spirit finely attuned to mine. No one knew more than she how desperately I tried to avoid surgery. She took a deep breath, dried her eyes and went about the business of making me comfortable. That was the last time I saw her cry.

In the middle of my fight for life, Cindy dropped by after she spoke to a ladies' meeting at the church. As always, I wanted to hear about her message.

As the ladies entered the room, Cindy asked each one to reach into a box, take a piece of a puzzle, and decide what part of the puzzle it was. The bits of cardboard were all shapes, sizes and colors. The ladies used their imaginations and each one announced to the others what her piece appeared to be. Some puzzle pieces were clearly parts of the foliage, sky, flowers, or the water, while other pieces were less obvious.

One lady declared, "This piece is nothing; just a dark, gray thing."

Anticipating such a comment, Cindy held up the picture on the box for all to see. It was a breathtaking scene, entitled "Rock of Ages." Cindy said, "Look! What you have in your hand is the very best part! You are holding a piece of the rock."

The dark piece was nothing pretty by itself. But when it was placed in its proper place within the whole picture, it suddenly had significance. The rock was the focal point. Without the dark pieces of the puzzle to make up the rock, the picture would have no significance.

Both the negative and the positive are essential to produce the power of electricity. Batteries have negative and positive poles. One without the other is useless. The two opposites work together. All things may not **be** good, but they work together for good.

> *...we know that all things work together for good to them that love God, to them who are the called according to his purpose.* (Romans 8:28 (KJV)

My very life was anchored to the Rock of Ages, not medical intervention. I was living on a promise and a prayer. Faith is real when it's all you have.

When all of the details were hammered out, the schedule for cancer treatments was to be administered in a different order than my first experience. Chemicals drastically weaken the body and mine had to be strong at the time of surgery for optimal recovery. Survival required every possible advantage. With that in mind, the doctors determined that I would undergo surgery first, followed by a small window of recovery. Chemotherapy treatments would begin as soon as I could tolerate them.

The date for surgery, December 10, 2003, was marked on the calendar and seared into my brain like a red-hot cattle brand. If all went well, I would be in the hospital for two weeks. That meant I would be home two days before Christmas. The holidays would be different on many levels.

Pre-registration papers and other details seemed to be repetitious of my previous bout with cancer and the surgery of December, 1994. Eventually, everything was set and I was prepared for radical pelvic exenteration...or was I?

Now faith is the substance of things hoped for, the evidence of things not seen. For by it the elders obtained a good testimony...But without faith it is

impossible to please Him, for he who comes to God must believe that He is, and that He is a rewarder of those who diligently seek Him.

(Hebrews 11:1,2, 6 - NKJV)

Hebrews 11 is known as the faith chapter of the Bible. Not one of the men or women of old, written about in the scriptures, had smooth sailing. They had assignments that were not easy. They endured afflictions and hardships, disappointments and persecution, suffering and desolation. What made them victorious and worthy of mention? It was their unwavering belief that God was faithful to His Word. Those faithful individuals saw beyond their temporary struggles. They simply believed and went into action. Their feats of victory have strengthened faint hearts for all time.

I set my sights beyond my present problem and I got a glimpse of victory.

P R A Y E R

ENVISION!

Eyes of faith behold what others never see.

There was a man who inherited a piece of ground that had been in his family for many years. It didn't seem fair that his portion had a huge mountain that prevented use of the acreage. He beseeched God to help him sell it, although he knew it was not a desirable piece of ground. He never stopped believing that God would somehow answer his prayer, even though his faith made him the laughing stock of the village. One day word came from the government that the stones and earth from his mountain were needed for landfill in the lowlands. Gigantic earthmoving equipment moved in and very soon the mountain was gone. The ground was finally level and of great worth. This man of prayer received sizeable compensation for a mountain that he did not want.

> *...if you have faith as a mustard seed, you will say to this mountain, 'Move from here to there,' and it will move; and nothing will be impossible for you.* (Matthew 17:20 & 21 - NKJV)

Prayer will move mountains out of your way. All you need is a mustard seed size portion of faith. Envision your mountain cast into the sea. The happiest people I know are those who exercise their measure of faith and see the victory through eyes of faith.

PRAYER: *Father, I resist the lies of the enemy. I know You have a plan and a reason for everything. Give me strength to stand on the Truth until the answer comes. Open the eyes of my heart to see that nothing is impossible with You...not mountains of fear, debt, sickness or doubt. You are my help in times of need. In Jesus' name, I pray.* Amen.

6

Rejoice!

*P*art of me wanted to wake up and part of me wanted to sink back into oblivion. My mind struggled to connect with the surroundings. The sounds made no sense. A clattering noise agitated me. A man was talking. Slowly my thoughts formed, just enough to know that I was not dreaming.

Where am I? What's going on? OH! I had surgery. I'm in the hospital.

At first, Dr. Polk's voice sounded far away. He was talking to Cindy. "Good news first: the tumor was contained. You might say it was encapsulated. Another good thing," Dr. Polk continued, "We only used one unit of blood. That's very good! We expected to use more...maybe four. Now, your mother may never walk again. We took so much out of her abdomen and I'm not certain if anything will ever stay in place. The innards, you know, they have to be *somewhere*. There's no way to connect a mesh shelf that would help support all that stuff. She may experience a great deal of pressure when she stands." Dr. Polk ended by saying, "It's not possible to predict what might happen. We never know, not with this one."

All those mortality warnings and the papers I had signed; I didn't hear a thing about not walking! This was probably something that was not expected. Something must have gone wrong. What did he mean? What is left inside of me?

I couldn't speak. I wanted to touch my stomach. I couldn't move my hands. I felt paralyzed. Then it hit me like a bolt of lightning; the antidote for the confusion.

Oh! He just said that the tumor was encapsulated. Encapsulated! I've been expecting that for a long time. I don't even care about all the other mumbo-jumbo that I couldn't understand. Praise the Lord!

God allowed me to hear those words of confirmation. That was exactly what Max, the dear brother in Christ back in Grand Prairie, Texas, had said: "The tumor is encapsulated!" It was exceptional news, although I couldn't speak a word at that moment.

As I slipped in and out of awareness, the doctor's comments concerning what might happen were not completely forgotten.

Doesn't Dr. Polk know that patients can hear conversations, even when they're drifting in and out?

Although I was disturbed by the doctor's remarks, it was meant to be that I overheard them. Righteous indignation, or maybe it was anger, arose from somewhere in the depths of the stupor. Then and there I made a silent decision.

God did not bring me through all this mud never to walk again. Lying flat on my back is not going to get it. Now, I have something to prove.

Finally, I opened my eyes and looked into Cindy's face. She asked, with a tinge of concern, "Mother, did you hear what the doctor said?" She hoped I had not. I found the strength to whisper my first words. "I heard. Don't worry. I'll out-shop you one of these days." The anxiety vanished and she laughed. Her mother might be down, but she was not out.

It bothers me to hear people say that God is good, just because something went their way. He is good...period. It is a fact, as sure as the law of gravity. Open the Bible and read about it on every page. His goodness was settled, once and for all, when Jesus died on the cross and rose again three days later. He redeemed my life and set my feet heavenward. The children of God have a win-win deal. I determined that, should I live, every day would count. What if I die? Well, that's the biggest win of all! I set my faith in agreement with the Word and my mind was made up. I would not allow the devil to steal one day of precious life that belonged to me.

God blessed Sarah with a child of promise when she was beyond childbearing age. Abraham received the promise and became the father of many nations. The God who never changes was able to heal me from this affliction. I am also a covenant woman with a promise. Emotions tend to vacillate, as mine did. A strong, determined mind is the key to living a life that brings honor to the Lord.

> *He [Abraham] staggered not at the promise of God through unbelief; but was strong in faith, giving glory to God; and being fully persuaded that, what he had promised, he was able also to perform. And therefore it was imputed to him for righteousness...* (Romans 4:20-22 – KJV)

The hustle and bustle of the holidays was in full swing outside the hospital and Christmas was in the air. As busy wives and mothers, Cindy and Suzanne were involved in church activities, school functions and children's programs. They had shopping to do and added responsibilities that go along with the season.

Every day I pleaded, "Cindy, please don't come to the hospital to spend the night. I'll be just fine." It was a 35-minute drive from her home to Baptist Hospital; however, when I heard her footsteps in the corridor every evening about 8:00, my heart leaped for joy. Cindy had the fortitude to see me with tubes all over my body. The ongoing functions that follow major surgery didn't seem to faze her. There was a constant stream of nurses attending to drainage bags and post-surgery needs. Cindy passed the hours by crocheting long neck wraps. All of the ladies on her gift list benefited from her vigils at the hospital. She hasn't picked up a needle since.

I developed a high fever and became very ill on the third night. I awakened Cindy and she notified the nurse, who immediately called Dr. Polk. He came into the room early the next morning and orders flew out of his mouth. As he examined the incision, Dr. Polk said to the nurse, "I've been afraid of this very thing happening."

I was not afraid. Remember? I had something to prove and some shopping to do.

The incision area turned red, indicating infection had set in. A four-inch opening in the incision had occurred above my waistline. The site had to be cleansed and packed with a special dark colored sponge that was connected to a vacuum machine. It drew out the inflammation from the area. Once that was accomplished the incision healed from the inside-out. In a few days the crisis passed. I was thankful to be rid of the noisy machine and the extra tube that went with it.

My greatest challenge from the beginning was preventing leakage at the site of the urostomy. An ostomy bag is usually connected to a small flange, known as a "wafer," which adheres to the person's skin. Its function is to maintain a watertight seal and it is supposed to be 100 percent leak proof. Mine was not. The adhesive backing lifted from my skin within minutes, causing the apparatus to be ineffective. My call light summoned the nurses almost every hour around the clock. They thought they had seen it all until I came along, but they were totally perplexed by this problem and never found a solution.

Nurses helped with the changing process in the hospital, but I was on my own at home. Nine years of experience with the colostomy helped. I had successfully adapted to it. The urostomy was altogether different.

Dr. Concepcion, the urologist who had removed the urinary bladder during surgery, had initially planned to perform what is known as an "ileal conduit urinary diversion." The procedure involves removing a small piece from the lowest part of the small intestine, known as the ileum. One end of that piece is then closed and the other end is connected to the outside of the abdomen, creating a sort of "mini-bladder." The tubes that drain urine from the kidneys, called ureters, are separated from the urinary bladder and then connected to a small section of the ileum. From there urine drains into a bag outside of the body. The procedure seemed like a medical marvel; almost too good to be true. It would have been sort of like having a small, surgically created bladder.

The surgery, however, didn't go as Dr. Concepcion had hoped. The size of the cancer was much bigger than previously thought, making it necessary to remove another six inches of the colon. There was not enough healthy tissue to perform the ileal diversion. Adding to the complications was the necessity of removing more of the ureters than expected. This necessitated placing the stoma in an area of the abdomen that prevented its flange from adhering to the skin. When this happens, the ostomy patient is virtually incapacitated, because of the constant leaking of urine at the site. Dr. Concepcion anticipated that I would have ongoing problems and sincerely regretted the unforeseen outcome. I was convinced that he did a superb job in spite of the situation and I appreciated his honesty.

The Enterostomal Therapy" (ET) nurses at Baptist Hospital are very competent professionals, but they were at their wits' ends with my unique problem. After trying all available products at the hospital, they could not produce a workable flange. Leaving the hospital was bittersweet. I had survived surgery. I could even see the hand of God in so many places. What I could not see was an answer for my problem, or way ever to live normally again.

The day I checked out of the hospital, I was advised to stop by Williams Medical Supply to get their advice. Hopefully, they would have a solution. Weak and dizzy, the last thing I wanted to do was to take a side trip on the way home.

Charlton was my representative at Williams. I had purchased ostomy supplies from him for the last nine years, but he had never encountered such a chronic leaking problem. He had no ready answer, but sold me another type of flange and crossed his fingers, hoping it would help. It turned out to be no different than the others. There was yet another box of expensive product on my shelf and one more item added to my does-not-work list.

The ongoing ostomy dilemma continued for five weeks. I was physically and mentally depleted. Five weeks felt like five eternities. I was dismayed by the long nights and too little sleep. The taste of hot, salty tears often awakened me. The reasons for crying were not always clear. Perhaps the medications had affected the balance of my nervous system, or it may have been the overwhelming sense of hopelessness. More likely, it was raw self-pity and a deep sense of loss. I was rapidly losing the desire to beat the odds or to face the light of another miserable day. I begged God to forgive me for praying to live. All I could see in the future was being held captive in my own home. My body was butchered by a surgery that left me empty, literally. The physical pain was real, but not as unbearable as the mental anguish. My faculties were intact and I was miraculously alive. I knew my name, but I no longer knew who I was.

I have known depressed people who wanted to die. Previous physical illnesses had never knocked me so far down. The first bout with cancer paled in comparison. During the long, despondent nights, I found a greater empathy for pathetic souls struggling with depression.

The Christmas tree was shimmering with beautiful white lights. Every nook and corner of the house reflected holiday bliss. The grandkids' stockings were hung on the mantle. I had tediously attended to these superficial aspects before I entered the hospital. Yet, the moment I returned home, harsh reality hit me in the face.

The not-so-obvious details of post surgery—the emotional aspects of my world—were in shambles. Oppression hovered over me like a smothering stench. All the lights in Nashville could not brighten the darkness. I felt trapped in the shadows of a decision made before the pain of loss set in.

Why did I sign that paper? I was braced for physical pain, but absolutely nothing had prepared me for this darkness.

Radical surgery always requires a long recovery. Drainage tubes, secured with stitches, protruded from my body. They were supposed to remain in place for 10 days, allowing the fluids to leave the incision site. The physical discomfort was not my greatest concern. The tubes would soon be gone, but I could not stay dry for even five minutes. Every move reminded me that nothing would ever be the same. I could not foresee normalcy in my life ever again. I wondered, "How can I live like this?" Hopelessness brought the onset of mental depression and threatened my very existence.

Diane, an ET nurse, advised me to resume my previous routine of irrigating the colostomy. Irrigating is a method of introducing water into the system, similar to an enema. The daily routine had served me well for nine years, preventing the need to wear a pouch or bag at the ostomy site. I had quickly embraced my new method of elimination. There are even advantages to having time control over bodily functions. After the second cancer surgery, however, the routine, to which I had become accustomed, mocked me.

Everything was different. Irrigating became another test of my endurance. It was one more reason to dread the mornings. Introducing the warm water into my digestive system made me nauseous the moment it entered my body, and I often blacked out. The new incision started five inches above my waist and extended vertically down my entire torso and around to the back. The metal staples and stitches made walking extremely difficult. A donut-shaped foam pillow enabled me to sit for only a few minutes at a time. Sleeping in a bed was not an option. I placed rubber-backed pads on a couch in the bedroom, where I spent elongated nights. I shall never forget how it feels to be out of control.

My brain must have deleted the information intended to prepare me for post-surgery conditions. I was trapped in a body that I did not recognize, did not like, and could not live with or without.

The adjustments to radical pelvic exenteration are more complicated than most other radical surgeries. It requires a big dose of sheer will power. The finality set in like an Amarillo blizzard. I had been cut open from top to bottom. The only parts that remained inside my body were vital organs—those absolutely essential for living—nothing more. I was physically traumatized and in a kind of shock. The ground seemed to be slipping away from underneath my feet. I was on a slippery slope and I could feel the downward pull. I did not know if I could hold on. I really did not know.

Loss of bodily function or the loss of any part of the anatomy often results in grief; it represents a kind of death. As humans, we are connected to our mortal flesh that gives us our unique identity. It's the house in which we live while on this earth; the vehicle by which we move and have our being. Reality blindsided me and it was too late. I surrendered my womanhood when I signed that consent paper. I lost everything on the operating table, except my ability to breathe and think. Admittedly, my perception was distorted, but that is exactly how I felt.

On the seventh day after coming home from the hospital, I told Levoy that I was on the verge of panic and something had to give. The one and only *tangible* thing that could possibly give was a stiff, red drainage tube that was stitched into the incision and poked me every time I moved. In total desperation, I announced, "I can't deal with this hideous thing another day! Are you going to help me, or am I going to do this myself?"

My soul-mate—my loving partner through this ordeal—was persuaded that any argument was pointless. When Levoy asked me what I wanted him to do, I handed him a little pair of scissors and pointed to a couple of stitches that were holding the annoying tube to my tummy. He snipped the black plastic thread and started pulling the red tube. It was not short, as I had supposed, but we were already committed and there was no turning back. The tube must have been at least 18 inches long!

Dr. Polk was very surprised at the next follow-up visit, when he saw that the drainage tube had been removed, but he didn't scold me. There were more important matters to discuss. I decided then that I liked the surgeon, including his blunt manner that occasionally rubbed me the wrong way. A little grin crept across his face when he heard my excuse about the tube: "I was fed up with that stupid thing." He shrugged his shoulders and said, "You are a spunky one. People like you seem to do pretty well."

A positive outcome of the surgery was the rapid and total healing of the incision. The doctor had forewarned me that the possibility of it completely closing was slim. Typically, there is ongoing seepage at the site, which necessitates wearing a dressing or pad. That was not the case and I felt extremely blessed. I had one more reason to rejoice!

After cancer number two and the problems with leakage, I lost a major portion of my dignity. I don't know of a better way to put it. Maybe it was only temporarily misplaced, but my usual sense of modesty was out the window. God did not let me die, so I had to find a way to live. In the struggle to solve my dilemma, I had very little embarrassment. You have probably heard the expression, "If Mama's not happy, ain't nobody happy!"

Almost everyone in my world got involved. One morning, I received a call from our 11 year-old grandson, Daniel. He blurted out the question on everyone's mind: "Mimi, are you dry?" Portia, Nathan's mom in California, was doing her own research for anything to hold an ostomy flange in place. My family, friends, and even some casual acquaintances were aware that I was in a bad situation and desperately crying out for help.

In spite of everything, we laughed a lot, just to keep from crying. I often said, "I sleep like a baby. Every three hours I wake up wet and crying." It was funny, but no joke. The obstacles following my surgery affected the entire family and they needed a break from the constant pressure.

Mark and Cindy made plans to take their three children on a picturesque, three-hour drive to Gatlinburg for Christmas. It was a much needed diversion for the holidays. On their way out of town they stopped by the house and Cindy made a brave attempt to comfort Levoy and me. "Next Christmas," she said, "we'll all go to Gatlinburg and lease a big chalet...like we've done before. We'll make up for this one. Just you wait and see."

I forced a smile, in an effort to appear enthused with her idea. The truth was that my mind defied looking that far ahead. The challenge of getting through the day was monumental. Sitting in the recliner with towels around me, I could not wrap my brain around packing a suitcase. I could not imagine planning a trip. How could I be anywhere except on these pads that held me like a prisoner?

Nathan, Suzanne and the boys flew to California to be with the Youngs for the holidays. Although it was a welcome break, the matters back at home overshadowed their visit.

On Christmas Day, Levoy took Mom and Dad Dewey to a lovely buffet at a downtown hotel. I was home alone for the first time. The house was deathly still. In an odd way, I welcomed the solitude, but my thoughts defied rest.

Is this the way the remainder of my life will be? What about future Christmases? Levoy deserves more. He is so sad and I cannot fix it. If I died, he could remarry.

Yes, it was a very different holiday.

I hated the aftermath of cancer. The disease had not killed me, but it was destroying all our lives. Something was terribly wrong with this picture.

What about the mud? When I had cancer before, I came to terms with it and finally embraced it, but this time I found myself sinking deeper and deeper into a slimy pit of hopelessness. The temptation to stop resisting tugged at me. Nothing had conditioned me to release my grip on life. I did not know how to stop fighting.

Everywhere I looked, it seemed as if Old Man Winter had come to stay; days were too short and nights were too long. It was near the end of February and spring would soon arrive, ushering in new life and new beginnings. Spring signifies change and I still believed the sun would shine again...someday.

Then it occurred to me: if all I have in this world is a promise, that's enough. Even in the darkness of uncertainty, seeds of hope were germinating in the midst of my mud. The undeniable conviction that God would not forsake me began to break through. I remembered His faithfulness. There had been too many confirmations, too many divine interventions to doubt His goodness. The key that would release me from virtual prison was soon to be placed in my hands.

A car door slammed outside my bedroom window. Before I could identify the vehicle through the tall trees in front of the house, I heard Nathan calling out to me, as he was walking down the hallway. By the pace of his steps, it was apparent that he had something important on his mind. My son-in-law had been on a mission to find a solution to my problem. He posed a question. "Mimi, have you ever thought about trying that gooey stuff? You know, the glue they use to stick on fake mustaches and beards for plays?" He went on before I could answer, "I was thinking, maybe that might work. I can run downtown to that costume shop on Church Street and buy some, if you'd like. It's worth a try, right?"

It didn't strike me as a reasonable solution at all. I replied, "Oh...I think that'd be too harsh for the skin. But thanks anyway."

After he left, Nathan's suggestion of using glue triggered my curiosity. The idea sounded completely irrational at first; then I reconsidered and possibilities started rolling around in my head. I had tried crazier things, so why not give it a shot? Nathan got me thinking "out of the box." I went to a drawer where some of my supplies were stored and started searching. I spied a product that had never been opened and I didn't have a clue what it was. The label on the container read, *"Skin Bond."* I picked up the metal jar, read the fine print and followed the instructions. Applying a small amount of the product to the adhesive backed flange totally changed everything. The problem was as good as solved, just that fast. As I learned to use it, I remained dry longer each day. Words are inadequate to describe my elation. It was almost an instantaneous transformation. Chains that held me were broken. I was miraculously set free by something that had been within reach all along: a simple can of glue.

The nightmare ended! I could make plans! I could function! I could live again! God had somehow granted special grace to bear the burden of dysfunction until the answer came. When my ability to cope was gone, God filled the void. His light penetrated the depths and miraculously transformed the darkness in my soul. It took a long time to see the miracle out of the mud. I had a strong, inner knowing that I had been spared by Almighty God for a definite purpose. Miracles often come in disguise and this one was covered with mud.

My oncologist, Dr. Spigel, projected that chemotherapy would begin in mid-January, a couple of weeks after my release from the hospital. When his office called, I flatly refused to book the appointment, much to the doctor's dismay. I said it was way too soon. Because of the dysfunctional urostomy, I had not made a final decision about going forward with chemotherapy. Thanks to answered prayer and *Skin Bond*, my state of mind made a 180-degree turn. Chemotherapy started in February.

Cancer patients are often given multiple chemotherapeutic agents with different properties to increase the chances of killing all the cancer cells. My "cocktail" combined three drugs: Oxaliplatin, Xolodin and Evastin. The latter was a trial drug that was approved by FDA shortly after my treatments concluded. A stack of papers had to be signed before taking the first treatment. The two-month schedule was two weeks on and two weeks off. The treatments were scheduled twice weekly and each drip took four hours to complete. A nurse charted every reaction and side effect in exhaustive detail.

Cindy set aside her regular pursuits of a home-based business, to drive and be with me at Sarah Cannon Research Center for the infusions. About an hour before the drip was finished, my body started twisting and contorting, as the muscles in my arms, hands, legs and feet hardened. It felt like my entire body was experiencing a Charlie-horse. I could not stand without support, and I had to be assisted out of the center and into the car. Xolodin caused excruciating sensitivity to cold and a sensation of pins and needles sticking my hands and feet. The trial drug, Evastin, brought about a myriad of side effects, including the cramping. These powerful chemicals were designed to be toxic to the disease; however, as they attack the cancer, they also play havoc on every other cell in the body. The discomfort persisted for about four days after each treatment and then diminished. I was almost free of the pain after the first two-week break. Too soon, however, it was time to go for another round.

Suzanne's life was totally consumed with attending to my needs for an entire year. She prepared meals and kept the house running smoothly. She only left me when she and Nathan had recording session work. I was the epicenter of her concerns. I sensed my children's presence in the room so many times. Their prayers echoed in my spirit through the late night hours. When my faith was weak, I depended on theirs.

At the half-way point in treatment, Levoy accompanied me to Sarah Cannon Research Center for a scheduled consultation with Dr. Spigel. The oncologist had asked me quite a few questions and now it was my turn. I had a very important, personal question to ask him at the right time and in private. The answer was for my ears only. I had no intentions of sharing this exchange between my doctor and me with anyone, including my husband. I did not expect Dr. Spigel's response to be encouraging, but I was already braced for another bad report. It would not be the first and my faith was fortified. I was not afraid to hear what he might say, because I knew there would be rejoicing in God's time.

When Levoy excused himself to move the car, I seized the moment for a one-on-one with Dr. Spigel. The rehearsed words spilled out of my mouth. "I have a question for you, while no one else is in the room. I want your honest opinion. Okay, here it is: how much time do I have?"

Dr. Spigel ended a long silence with these words: "It's probably not what you would like to hear. You asked for my honest opinion, so here it is: I believe this cancer will kill you...eventually."

In a whisper, I asked, "How long do you think it will take?"

The doctor replied softly, mirroring my tone, "You might have as long as a year. It depends on how well you respond to the drugs. Given your overall health, we have reason to be somewhat hopeful. However, you could expire in as little as three months...six months. We just don't know."

I didn't flinch. I heard the prognosis first hand and it was very clear. From that day forward, I had no doubts about where my oncologist stood. My immediate and unwavering statement had not been rehearsed. It came from the depths of my soul. "I'll do everything in my power to prove you wrong. A lot of prayers are going up for me."

Levoy reentered the room and the subject was conveniently changed. I promised myself that I would never tell him about this, because I knew it would break his heart; however, something inside me snapped the second we exited the building and it all came pouring out. I could not stop the torrent of words, emotions, and bitter tears.

We had been married way too long to hide our feelings. His attempt to be brave was honorable. He thought going out to lunch would be a good idea. Perhaps doing something normal would make us both feel better. At our favorite Chinese restaurant, near the hospital, we took a table in the corner away from other diners. I hoped no one saw me crying.

Entering the infusion room never failed to shock me. The smell of the chemicals hit my senses before I reached the swinging glass doors. I went through this ordeal nine years before, but I never got used to seeing so many sick people in one place. The large room was completely filled with recliners, where cancer patients sat and received their treatments. Each one was situated near a small table and a metal stand that supported the bags of chemicals. Clear plastic tubing carried the powerful drugs into veins.

The saddest patients, in my estimation, were the young people. Even now, their faces flash before me. There were college students, young mothers and dads, too many in their prime. I was touched by their gutsy fight for a life they desperately longed to live. When I considered the contrast of my age to theirs, I felt largely blessed. In that setting, I became cognizant that I was living on borrowed time. Deep within I knew that my days--that all our days—were not borrowed, but divinely ordained by an all-wise God.

And in Your book they all were written, the days fashioned for me, when as yet there were none of them. (Psalm 139:16 - NKJV)

Dr. Spigel forewarned me that my hair would fall out at a specific time. With that in mind, Nathan took me to a beauty supply and helped me select a stylish wig. It waited on my dressing table, ready to go on my soon-to-be bald head. A new haircut was extremely short to help ease the shock. Everything was ready for the inevitable.

On the way to one of my treatments, Cindy casually mentioned that Peggy Branhan was praying that I would not lose my hair. It touched my heart that this intercessor at the church was so concerned about that particular aspect. I said, "How nice. Be sure and tell Peggy that I really appreciate her prayers and concern about my hair." Her caring exemplified a discerning, sensitive spirit. However, I was not really worried about the hair. It would grow back. I just wanted to live.

The week arrived when I was supposed to lose my hair; Dr. Spigel knew when it would likely happen. I sat in his office for my evaluation when he entered the room. He turned to take a second look at me. He reached over and tugged at my short hair, looking a bit puzzled. "You got your hair cut again, didn't you?" He asked. "This is really unusual," he said. "You haven't lost your hair." Dr. Spigel immediately saw it as a rare event, given the drugs I was taking. He concluded, "I don't expect it will happen at this point...not now."

I soon came to appreciate the significance of this blessing. As the weeks proceeded and the side effects of chemo worsened, I was thankful that I didn't have to don the wig.

God is always up to something, with you and me in mind.

Until the hair thing, I tried so hard to "do it right." God had brought me through cancer before. I was in a strange, yet familiar place. So, I tried to pray like I prayed before. I tried to read the same scriptures as before. I tried to say the same things I said before. It turned out so well the first time, I tried for a repeat. At times I felt guilty, because all my trying was not enough. Perhaps, I thought, I didn't do all the right things on a particular day, or maybe I hadn't tried hard enough. Then I felt badly that I had not done more. I tried again and again. It was a self-imposed burden that was too much for me to carry.

When my hair stayed firmly planted on my head, despite the certain predictions of the oncologist, I learned a valuable lesson: I did not *have* to bear a burden that Jesus had placed on *someone else's* heart. I didn't have to have *all* the faith. Peggy was praying for me and others were praying for me too. God was speaking to *them* about *my* needs and I was not alone.

Bear ye one another's burdens, and so fulfill the law of Christ. (Galatians 6:2 - KJV)

I relaxed. There were many days when I was too weak to pray, too sick to read the Bible or quote a litany of scriptures. There were times when I could hardly speak; all I could do was whisper, "Lord I trust You." The most effective prayers are desperate pleas from the heart and sometimes they are inaudible. A whispered prayer is thunderous in God's compassionate ear.

> **Therefore my heart is glad and my glory rejoiceth: my flesh also shall rest in hope.**
>
> (Psalms 16:9 - KJV)

I had waded through the mud of radical surgery, the needles of chemotherapy, and an important date with the doctor was approaching. I was more than a little apprehensive about this particular meeting, when a full evaluation by the Tumor Board would be disclosed. I entered the room with head held high, armed with faith, expecting something good to happen.

Dr. Spigel walked into the room where Cindy, Levoy and I were waiting. We were poised to hear the verdict. The doctor wore a big grin...something I had not seen heretofore. I felt better already. He held a few sheets of paper, rolled up in his hand. As he began to speak, he enthusiastically tapped the papers in the palm of his other hand. Still grinning, he said, "I never thought I would see you sitting here today. And I never thought—not in a million years—that I'd be saying what I am about to tell you. The Tumor Board and I can find no disease in your body." Dr. Spigel's voice proclaimed firmly, "There's no cancer; nothing whatsoever wrong with you!"

Tucked inside my memory were Dr. Polk's warnings of the alarming mortality of radical pelvic exenteration. And here we were, hearing the best news this side of Heaven. Dr. Spigel mused, "You've survived more cancer than anyone I've ever seen. We are making a new file on your case. There's no other reference like yours at this point."

The energy of his exuberance charged the room. What an amazing report! After a time of talking and letting the news soak in, I asked, "Do I need to take any medicine...you know, prescriptions?" I had been taking a ton of drugs.

Dr. Spigel shook his head and smiled, "Why do you need medicine? There's nothing wrong with you." He continued, "You will need to have regular check-ups and an MRI every six months for a couple of years, then annually for a while. We'll make those calls as we go. That's it."

My heart was rejoicing! I was singing a new song of praise to the One who does all things well. At last, I had reached the pool. I had prayed for this day and imagined how it would feel to hear the doctor say those words. I was basking in the sunshine of a *positive* life-changing event. At last, I had broken through the dry, hard crust of very deep mud!

Three extremely happy people followed the doctor into another room. We posed for pictures with him and the attending nurses. They handed me a Certificate of Completion that bore a gold seal from the Sarah Cannon Research Center of Centennial Hospital. One of the pictures was attached to the paper. The doctor expressed regrets that more of these awards were not given. Many of the personnel in the offices came around to congratulate me. One receptionist asked, "Do you really get it, what a big deal this certificate is?"

Oh yes, I got it! April 22, 2003 was a joyous day I shall never forget. One of the pictures was tacked to the bulletin board at Sarah Cannon, along with others who completed the program. Everyone who walked into the treatment room would see the big smile on my face. My long battle with recurring colorectal cancer was over. The storm passed. The mud of cancer was gone. In my hand was a piece of paper. It bore the profound statement from the medical community that agreed with the words of my mouth.

My prayer was answered and the medical community of Nashville finally knew it. I was the MIRACLE out of the MUD!

A feeling of unspeakable gratitude washed over me. I wanted to run outside and shout in the streets, "Hey, everybody! Look at me! I am going to live!" I was the woman in hopeless condition, given up for certain death. I walked out of the doctor's office with a clean bill of health. For the rest of my life, there will be no doubt: the rest of my days belong to God.

The role medicine played in the healing process cannot be disregarded or belittled in any way. More than ever, I was grateful for every nurse and every doctor, for their depth of medical knowledge and skill; grateful for the comfortable facility; the diligent research by dedicated and caring people. All of these factors made a huge contribution to the best possible outcome. I will ever esteem the part they played in my restored health. I wrote letters of thanks to everyone, but never lost focus of the truth: thirty-nine stripes on the bleeding back of my Savior bought healing. The glory belongs to the One who paid the ultimate price.

The blind man was no less healed because of the mud. I was no less healed because of the surgery and chemotherapy. Jesus is the healer of all our ills and He uses any means he chooses, for His purpose.

To everything there is a season, and a time to every purpose under the heaven: A time to be born, and a time to die; a time to plan, and a time to pluck up that which is planted; A time to kill, and a time to heal; a time to break down, and a time to build up; A time to weep, and a time to laugh; a time to mourn, and time to dance; A time to cast away stones, and a time to gather stones together; a time to embrace, and time to refrain from embracing; A time to get; and a time to lose; a time to keep, and a time to cast away; A time to rend, and a time to sew; a time to keep silence, and a time to speak; A time to love, and time to hate; a time of way, and a time of peace.

I know that there is no good in them, but for a man to <u>*rejoice,*</u> *and to do good in his life.*

(Ecclesiastes 3:1-8, 12 - NJKV)

The twelfth verse is seldom quoted, yet it is the most important one in the chapter. Solomon said there is no good to be found in deed or emotion, without rejoicing. That's what I was missing. When I stopped rejoicing, depression took me for a wild ride. Rejoicing completed the picture and it was a beautiful thing. The season of weeping had finally passed. The time for rejoicing was here!

It had been a long life-changing process. Most of all, I regretted my family's sacrifices. There were tears of unspeakable joy in my eyes, mingled with a deep sadness. Life had passed me by. Months of dealing with health issues had turned into years. I looked around and recognized that my absence had created a void. I had been there, but distracted. The little ones did not stop growing until I got better. While I fought for life, I missed a lot of birthdays, school plays, graduations, attending church, times when I may have failed to recognize their accomplishments. Watching the grandchildren grow has been a treasure in my heart that shall never be taken for granted. I hope they understand and pray that they don't resent the times I could not be there when they needed me. I had a lot of catching up to do, but I could have missed it all.

Our youngest grandchild, Benjamin, is a gentle reminder that God really cares about our concerns. Suzanne started losing amniotic fluid in her sixth month. During the delivery there was a real crisis, with the presence of meconium. How thankful we are for answered prayers and the good care she and the baby received. This strong, healthy child has a big heart of love and is generously blessed with gifts of music and mercy. Just as we rebuked the mud of cancer, we stood against the demise of our joy.

Cancer robbed me of many things, but I gained even greater wealth. Through the "mudding" process, I discovered a place of refuge in the eye of the storm. Whenever the world is falling apart, a sanctuary is waiting in His everlasting arms.

You may look around and see seeds that have died. It doesn't matter. When God shines His light upon you, no amount of mud can hold you down. You may be the only one to survive. The "mud" will provide the perfect environment for your germinating process.

When I fought the mud, I sank deeper. I had to embrace the mud to get through it. So, don't be afraid to give God your mud. Mud in His hands is raw material with which He creates miracles. You will receive so much more than the mess you gave Him. You can trust Him.

The hand of God was obvious in my mud. I didn't need a bolt of lightning to get the message, to hear an audible voice or see writing on the wall. My life had been given back to me. Looking back at the devastation, I could see the big picture. The mud had a purpose. The call of God is without repentance. He had not changed His will because of a thing called cancer. There were yet more miles to travel, hearts to encourage and hope to offer other hurting souls. What was intended for evil, God used for my good and for His Glory.

> *But as for you, you meant evil against me; but God meant it for good, in order to bring it about as it is this day, to save many people alive.*
>
> (Genesis 50:20 - NKJV)

The message of Genesis 50:20 is relevant today. I am living proof of it. My part was simple: surrender the process to Him.

> *So shall My word be that goes forth from My mouth; It shall not return to Me void, but it shall accomplish what I please, and it shall prosper in the thing for which I sent it. For you shall go out with joy, and be led out with peace; the mountains and hills shall break forth into singing before you, and all the trees of the field shall clap their hands.*
>
> (Isaiah 10:11-12 - NKJV)

Levoy and I were in Dr. Spigel's office on the first year anniversary of my clean bill of health. I had an MRI earlier that day, and the usual follow-up lab work had been completed. The doctor reviewed the numbers and checked the results from the imaging department. Dr. Spigel greeted us pleasantly and said, "You are an amazing lady. Just to think that your chances of survival were not good. Now, a year after the fact, you're still here and have no signs of cancer." The doctor paused for emphasis, "Just to remind you, three to five out of 1,000 make it through that surgery. Only one out of 5,000 reach the point where you are now, with good quality of life." Dr. Spigel smiled and said, "By the way, I have a brand new word in my vocabulary."

Curiously, I asked, "What is the word?"

He looked at me with a broad smile across his face and replied, "You are...'*it*.'"

"Miracle" is a wonderful word to have in one's vocabulary!

*P   R   A   Y   E   **R***

REJOICE!

Rejoicing is an expression of the soul that has little to do with circumstance.

Many of the Apostle Paul's letters to the churches were written from prison. Imagine Paul and Silas joyously singing in a Roman jail; the earth shaking; miraculous deliverance from bondage; the apostle's ever present "thorn in the flesh"; the uncommon anointing that was upon Paul to preach Christ; his timeless epistles written while in chains.

Exultation to the Most High, while enduring deprivation and pain, gets God's undivided attention. He will show up for you, too. Rejoicing in dismal conditions is true praise.

In everything give thanks; for this is the will of God in Christ Jesus concerning you.
(I Thessalonians 5:18 - KJV)

Anything that stops your rejoicing stands between you and God. The enemy will use that very thing to make you ineffective. Thanksgiving will produce answers to prayer, put everything in the right order, and draw others to the Lord. You will be successful and find happiness.

Rejoice in the Lord always. Again, I say rejoice!
(Philippians 4:4 – NKJV)

PRAYER: *My Lord, My God and my Redeemer, I rejoice today because of who You are. May the meditations of my heart and the words of my mouth be acceptable in Your courts. Praise and worship are my most powerful weapons. I will never, ever stop rejoicing!* Amen.

Inspirational
MUD BABY Stories

*M*ud comes in many colors, shapes and sizes; it affects all ages, races, and both genders. Mud may look like lost hopes, shattered dreams, or any hard place. Cancer is not the most devastating thing that can happen to someone, although it does get one's attention. If I have elevated that disease as the worst, I have failed. Cancer was my burden. Yours may be quite different. As you have read, my spiritual eyes began to see life's problems as mud. More importantly, I saw beautiful things springing forth from the midst of the mud that threatened my life.

Broken relationships are heartbreaking and Christian homes are certainly not exempt. The deceiver slips up on the blind side. He is aware of the places that are not covered by the blood of Christ. Pray for discernment in recognizing delusion and for the wisdom to deal with it.

Being falsely accused produces emotional injury. Betrayal by one who once held your trust is the pain of real mud. Maintaining your faith when you have been maligned is one of the greatest tests.

Throughout many years in the ministry, I have spoken with countless women who have been abused, misused, and discarded. They deal with unresolved anger and misplaced guilt. Personal violations and other crimes leave permanent damage, until they are surrendered to the great Healer.

I can think of no heavier burden than unforgiveness. It is a spiritual cancer that overtakes and destroys all the good. Forgiving another person is an act of self-preservation. Forgiving oneself is often a more difficult task, but every bit as necessary. Bearing the heavy burden of past mistakes is nonproductive. God forgives and forgets.

The wisdom of God enables us to conquer the issues of life and death. Give your destruction to the Lord and experience His grace in action. Only He can mend the wounds of fragmented lives, and no life is broken beyond repair. From the dust of the earth we were created and the dirt from whence we came is all around us. When we depart this life, we return to dust.

We are all Mud Babies!

I have long been inspired by *Mud Babies*; the people who emerge as victors from their most serious challenges. Somewhere between the mud and the pool, victorious *Mud Babies* realize that their ultimate purpose is greater than their present circumstances.

Here are some inspirational stories from *Mud Babies* I know (some of the names in their stories have been respectfully changed). Read to the end to find out how you can contribute your own *Mud Baby* story!

*D*ebbie was 16 when she attended a Youth Camp where we were scheduled to minister and sing for a week. She did not participate in the activities of the camp. Something about her disquieted me. I made repeated efforts to talk with her, desiring to bring her out of her shell. One day she finally opened up and the story that poured out of her broken heart was stunning.

Debbie confided that her Dad had sexually molested her since she was five years old. In her desperate attempt to mask the pain, she got into drugs and a promiscuous lifestyle. What made matters even worse, Debbie's mother refused to confront incest within the family. The details were later confirmed by someone who knew the family's history.

A concerned friend convinced Debbie to come to the Youth Camp. There she surrendered her life to the Lord and began to find peace of mind. Debbie had a journey ahead, along a rocky road, as she worked through intense hostility. Triumph came when she was able to forgive those who had betrayed her trust.

Since that pivotal experience at a Youth Camp, Debbie has lived a productive, victorious life. This lovely young woman, once damaged and broken, is an active member of a thriving church and is a blessing to many.

*T*he telephone rang at midnight, during the same week I was diagnosed with cancer. On the other end of the line was the familiar voice of a close friend. I heard the pain in her trembling voice. She had discovered love letters in her husband's brief case from another woman. There had been other signs of an extramarital relationship, but this was undeniable evidence.

The husband soon left my friend and their two young sons, and took a job in a faraway city. Although she was devastated, my friend tried desperately to hold her family together. In her heart, she did not want the divorce that appeared inevitable. Their church family and friends prayed for God's intervention.

Not long after the separation, she received an unexpected phone call from her husband. He told her that he had advanced cancer of the mouth.

Everything changed suddenly. My friend and their sons traveled to be present during surgery. A year later, the marriage was reconciled, but the cancer returned. They faced a grim prognosis with a second surgery, a radical neck resection.

This caring wife and mother had tremendous compassion for her husband, and when he passed away a few months later, my friend had peace of mind. Although it was not easy, she knew she had done the right thing. Her sons will never forget her thoughtfulness. In caring for her husband during his last days on earth, she found closure to the pain that otherwise could have destroyed her.

Forgiveness became practical and loving action. Resentment would have been a high price to pay. The thorn of bitterness never dies of its own volition; it must be plucked out decisively. The scars of a broken home were healed when forgiveness and obedience opened the door.

*M*arcie was a beautiful, talented young girl, the daughter of a successful business-man, who enjoyed the luxuries of a charmed life...or so it seemed. Marcie's life started spiraling downward when she went away to college, fell into the wrong crowd and started using marijuana and other illicit drugs. It was fun to live on the edge at first, but it quickly became a noose around her neck.

One poor choice led to another. Her boyfriend convinced her that having a child would be an inconvenience and that abortion was the sensible solution. Sadly, a botched procedure left her unable to bear any children. The heartbroken young girl carried the shame of her dark secret like a stone in her heart.

Eventually, Marcie fell in love and got married, but she never had the courage to divulge the mistakes of her past to her husband, who wanted to be a dad more than anything in the world. At last, Marcie was forced to reveal the truth. The marriage ended in a bitter divorce, because of her deceit and the distrust it fostered.

At the age of 23, Marcie found herself at rock bottom. Her addictions included cutting her body, which indicated unresolved self-hate.

God did not give up on Marcie, although she had given up on herself. I lost contact and was unaware of her difficulties until she reappeared at one of our services in Florida. We learned that Marcie had remarried and was the happy mother of two adopted children. The golden opportunity of saving two babies, who were scheduled for abortion, was the gateway to redeem past mistakes.

How delighted we were to hear this victorious outcome; proof that no life is broken beyond repair.

*L*evoy was Music Director for a large church in Florida, until the pastor dismissed him abruptly from his duties. We knew it was the push we needed to commence our traveling ministry, and over the next 10 years, we responded to several invitations to return for special services. The congregation always welcomed us with open arms. Although the past was never discussed and our fellowship was cordial, the pain of being uprooted was fresh in our minds when we arrived for a District Council in Tampa, Florida.

I addressed the women in one of the morning sessions. It was my first opportunity to tell the story of surviving cancer and I was apprehensive about divulging personal aspects of my life. Sister Brown, our former pastor's wife, sat toward the back of the large room. I couldn't help noticing that she did not make eye contact with me throughout my testimony. There were approximately 75 ladies present that morning, so I focused on others.

I prayed with several women at the conclusion of the session. It was a time of blessing, and a sense of liberation came over me that morning. I was free to be transparent, no longer bound by fear.

Sister Brown's demeanor still puzzled me. She suffered with severe arthritis, so I reckoned that her lack of response was unintentional. As I collected my things and prepared to leave the room, I felt a hand on my arm. I turned and looked into the troubled eyes of this dear lady. She began pouring out her heart through her tears. "I cannot look at you," she cried. "Every time I hear your name, I feel just terrible about your leaving the church. We did not treat you right and I'm so miserable. Carrying this guilt is killing me. Will you please forgive us?"

At that moment, I knew why I had been asked to speak that day. God put words in my mouth and empathy in my heart. I quietly embraced the sobbing body of a sister in the Lord for a long moment. Finally, I said, "The last thing I want is for you to ever feel guilty about our leaving the church. It was God's time for us to launch the ministry of evangelism. I was the one holding back. God used you to get us out the door. I want to take this burden off your shoulders, once and for all. Levoy and I love you both very much."

Sister Brown let out a big sigh of relief. Her bright blue eyes were shining when, half laughing, half crying, she said, "Thank you! Thank you so much. We love you, too."

That conversation could have taken place long before that day, but I admired the courage it took to confront the ugly face of guilt and condemnation. The air was cleared by a simple gesture of humility. Communication liberated two souls that morning, and two friends left the room with lighter steps and lifted spirits. I learned a valuable lesson about communication and the pleasant afterglow of forgiveness.

*M*ud Babies cover a wide spectrum of age, appearance, gender and creed. As long as you have the breath to fog a mirror, you will be a *Mud Baby*. That fact is emphasized every time I visit the nursing home where Mom Dewey resides. It is not where she would choose to spend her "golden years," but God planted her to bloom in the middle of a mission field. Thankfully, Mom Dewey still commands her mental faculties and is a witness for Christ in the facility. Although her ninety-plus year-old body is wearing out, her zeal for Christ has not waned. She often prays for those around her who are suffering paranoia, dementia, loneliness and physical dysfunction. Her

God-given desire to hang on and not lose another inch of ground is admirable.

Everyone alive approaches a day of sweet release. A time comes when the pull of tomorrow's Heaven is stronger than life itself. The gradual letting go of this earth is God's way of preparing His dear ones for the moment when we sail away to be with Him.

Those in their twilight season are still going through mud. These seasoned warriors have weathered the winds of many storms and dealt with their muddy aftermath. I empathize with those silver-haired *Mud Babies*.

*F*or many years, we kept a snapshot of a tiny baby girl on our refrigerator. She was connected to all kinds of tubes and the picture served as a gentle reminder that someone I loved needed a lot of prayer. This little angel had intelligent eyes that could not be forgotten. Everyone who came into the kitchen saw the image of the infant and wanted to know the story behind the picture.

Jamie Lee Johnson was the granddaughter of Clois and Nancy Cotton, my brother and sister-in-law. The call I awaited, announcing the baby's birth, was laced with many concerns. Mental retardation and the absence of kidneys was only the beginning of a long list of abnormalities, about which the doctors had already informed Jamie Lee's parents, Bobbie and Benny. Thankfully, those suspicions proved false, but a diagnosis of cystic fibrosis was confirmed. The baby, accompanied by her mother, had to be flown 130 miles by helicopter from Amarillo to Lubbock, Texas. There she remained at a specialized neonatal unit for many weeks.

Whenever the doctors announced more alarming information, more prayers ascended. Tiny Jamie Lee beat the odds time after time in her valiant fight, and what a fighter she was! There were countless hospital stays and surgeries throughout her youth, in addition to ongoing crises concerning her medication and breathing problems. An endless battery of tests and treatments were the norm. Almost every week there was another trauma.

When Jamie was 15 years old, she received the trip of her life from the Make-A-Wish Foundation. She had the joy of accompanying her entire family to Disney World in Orlando.

When I consider the stories of *Mud Babies* that have made the most profound impressions on me, Jamie Lee comes to mind. She gave her heart to Jesus at a very young age and trusted Him for every breath she took. It was touching to know how she encouraged her loved ones to invite Him into their hearts as well.

Jamie wearied from her struggle, and an oxygen tank sustained her. It was not possible for her to run and play, like her sister and her cousins, but she did not complain. My little great-niece was a hero to everyone who knew her.

The mud that Jamie went through, during her brief life, seems entirely unfair. I believe with all my heart that those who witnessed her journey—or even heard about—were changed. I certainly was. I also know that her Paw-Paw and Granny wore out some carpet in their home, while on their knees in prayer on Jamie's behalf.

If Jamie could speak to us now, I believe she would say, "Don't worry about the mud of cystic fibrosis. I have seen Jesus and that's all that really matters."

*L*evoy and I were in Enid, Oklahoma, for a three-day revival in the spring of 1999. Our little grandson, Andrew, was three years old at the time and it seemed an opportune time to bring him along on the bus with his Mimi and Poppy. He was adorable, with his reddish blonde hair and big brown eyes. His cute conversation and games made the trip from Nashville a lot more fun.

The revival started on Sunday and on Monday afternoon we heard the storm warning beep on the television. The crawl at the bottom of the screen said that conditions were favorable in the Enid area for tornadoes. Soon after we arrived at the church, Pastor Poldson informed us that several funnels had been spotted on the outskirts of town. We gathered in the sanctuary, along with a few of the church folks who dared to venture out, and prayed for the safety of those in harm's way. The Pastor wisely dismissed everyone to seek shelter. The church was empty within a few minutes.

Levoy, Andrew and I jumped in the car with the Pastor and his wife, Faye. It was obvious immediately that it was not safe to travel across town to their house. The radio warned people to stay off the streets and reported that a funnel had touched down on the outskirts of the city.

We quickly found shelter under a brick awning of a Baptist church. It seemed that we sat there a long time, waiting and praying. Little Andrew couldn't understand why we didn't go to McDonald's and watch the big storm from there. Troubling thoughts danced in my head, knowing the real-life drama that played only a short distance away. We were helpless and at the mercy of God. Oh, how we prayed!

The next morning we beheld the sunny sky and were thankful to be safe. When we turned on the television, the following report, from the local newspaper, was the top story.

Saturday, May 8, 1999 – Enid News & Eagle

"I just kept telling her to keep crying"

*Deputy recalls thrill of finding baby
in rubble left by tornado!*

CHICKASHA (AP) Next to the tree, something caught Deputy Robert Jolley's eye. "Maybe it's just a shirt," he thought. But then it moved.

He walked closer and saw brown, curly hair sticking out of the red Oklahoma mud. "No, it's a baby...a silent baby."

Jolley couldn't even feel the chicken wire and wooden boards poking him as he dug through the tornado destruction Monday night. He just wanted to get the little baby in blue overalls. Finally, he reached her. She was still warm. He thought, "She's not crying. Why isn't she crying?"

Her little eyes and ears were packed in mud. He started to dig. Thoughts of his, own 18-month-old daughter, Tia, made his heart race faster.

"I just started removing the dirt from her eyes, then she cried," Jolley said, "I never thought I would be so happy to hear a baby screaming."

The 27-year-old Grady County deputy, in brown Wranglers, carried 10-month-old Aleah Crago to his patrol vehicle. A video camera in the dash board taped the little girl's screams and outreached arms, begging for comfort. It showed Jolley's standard officer frisk, looking for injuries, and then his father's response to just hug the child.

Aleah was found about 100 feet from the closet in which she was hiding with her parents and grandparents near Bridge Creek when Monday's tornado ripped through. Her grandmother died. Her father was listed in critical condition Friday. And her mother and grandfather escaped with bruises and cuts.

Aleah just had a hairline fracture and a cut on her head. "A true miracle baby," Jolley said.

The first year deputy was following the twister's destruction path when he spotted people wandering on a country road. Robert Williams, the baby's grandfather, told Jolley and other searchers that he lost his kids.

He said, "They blew right out of the roof." Jolley said, "When we heard that one of the missing was a baby, the real search began."

After Jolley found Aleah, he waited for emergency workers until he couldn't take it any longer. He jumped in his vehicle with the baby in his lap, her head on his chest, and drove.

"I just kept telling her to keep crying," he said. About 45 minutes later he found help at a makeshift hospital at a school. "It's a good thing we ran into EMS because I would've kept her. We would've gone right home," Jolley joked.

He turned the baby away from him so he wouldn't have to see her face as he handed her to a worker.

"I just couldn't take it," he said. "I don't like emotional things."

Jolley told the guys later that his contacts were acting up to explain his red, moist eyes.

When he got home the next morning he headed right into Tia's room. "I just saw my baby," he said.

Jolley still didn't know Aleah's name on Friday. He hasn't seen her since that night, but he would like to someday.

The rescue video from his patrol car is shown upon request. "It's a moment caught on tape I will always keep and hope I never have to repeat," he said.

When he got home, Jolley said, "Whenever Tia, my daughter, is crying, I just cheer her on."

It has been documented that the baby was saved by a cushion of mud.

The tornado broke up a lot of property and hurt some innocent people. It also left a lot of mud in its wake. On the other hand, the mud provided a safe landing for the baby at the end of her swift exit through the roof of her house. God prepared a soft place to fall for a little baby in Enid.

God reaches way down into the mire and rescues Mud Babies from the storms of life. We may not look so good, but He knows all the potential hidden in all that mess. He cleans us up and clothes us in new garments; in robes of righteousness. Can you remember a time when you went through something really awful, but in the end it turned out for your good? He loves us just the way He finds us, but He never leaves us in the same condition.

God lovingly wipes the tears from the weeping eyes of His dear Mud Babies.

What's your *MUD BABY story?*

Your life-changing, faith-affirming experience could be included in the upcoming book,
Mud Baby Stories.

Find out more. Write to us at...

info@MiracleoutoftheMud.com

Addendum

66 Verses from Books of the Bible

*P*lease don't lay the book aside unfinished. This final section is the best; the tools to dig a miracle out of the mud.

My words are from a human perspective, but the words from the Bible will never return void. On my desk is an old King James Version that I've read through several times during the past 30 years. Hand-written dates and personal notes fill the frayed margins around the scriptures printed on its yellowed pages. The truths that follow are the treasures of my faith. The Bible is my compass on rough, uncharted waters. It is my root and the bedrock of my life. Its timeless wisdom has sustained Levoy and me through every crisis and given direction for raising our children. When we failed, the Word of God was the rudder that brought our vessel back on course.

I pray the Lord will heal your wounds and touch your scars, as surely as He has mine. There are answers to the issues of spirit, mind, soul and body. If your body is well and your mind is sick, you are fragmented. Open your heart and allow God's Word to make you whole, in Jesus' name.

All of the following are from the New King James Version.

1) Genesis 50:20

But as for you, you meant evil against me; but God meant it for good, in order to bring it about as it is this day, to save many people alive.

The thread of truth starts in the first book of the Bible and runs through Revelation. God can turn anything into a blessing...even cancer.

2) Exodus 15:26

...I am the Lord who heals you.

"I AM" will never change. Medical science has its place. It is God who opens man's understanding to all knowledge. Healing is a gift from God, no matter how it comes.

3) Leviticus 26:6

And I will give peace in the land, and you shall lie down, and none will make you afraid...

When sleep is denied, a sound mind and good health are often compromised. There is rest for the children of the Lord...and no fear.

4) Numbers 23:19

God is not a man, that He should lie, Nor a son of man, that He should repent. Has He said, and will He not do it? Or has He spoken, and will He not make it good?

Confidently stand on God's Word...every promise, every correction, every truth. It is infallible. God will not...God cannot fail!

5) Deuteronomy 28:13

And the Lord will make you the head and not the tail; you shall be above only, and not be beneath...

This is the joy of covenant. No matter what the circumstance, rise above it in the favor of God.

6) Joshua 24:15

...choose for yourselves this day whom you will serve...But as for me and my house, we will serve the Lord.

Levoy and I made the choice to position ourselves and our household on the Lord's side. That decision gives you authority to claim your rightful inheritance.

7) Judges 2:1

...I led you up from Egypt and have brought you to the land which I swore to your fathers; and I said, I will never break My covenant with you.

We are joint-heirs to every blessing of God. His sacred covenant is eternally written in the blood of Jesus.

8) Ruth 1:16

But Ruth said, Entreat me not to leave you, or turn back from following after you: for wherever you go, I will go; and wherever you lodge, I will lodge: your people will be my people, and your God my God.

By way of salvation, the Kinsman Redeemer (the Lord) will ever be our covering. He will take care of us.

9) I Samuel 16:7

...For the Lord does not see as man sees; for man looks at the outward appearance, but the Lord looks at the heart.

God knows the intent of your heart. You cannot hide from Him. You need never be concerned about being misunderstood by Him.

10) II Samuel 22:4

I will call upon the Lord, who is worthy to be praised; so shall I be saved from my enemies.

Our most powerful weapon is praise! It confuses the enemy when we honor Almighty God.

11) I Kings 18:21

...How long will you falter between two opinions?

An unstable mind will cause failure. God, help us never doubt You.

12) II Kings 20:5

...I have heard your prayer, I have seen your tears; surely I will heal you...

No "if" or "maybe" in this promise. He WILL heal. The timing is His, not ours.

13) I Chronicles 4:10

And Jabez called on the God of Israel, saying, "Oh that You would bless me indeed, and enlarge my territory, that Your hand would be with me, and that You would keep me from evil, that I may not cause pain!" So God granted him what he requested.

Jabez' name means "trouble." He overcame his name with this short prayer.

14) II Chronicles 7:14

If My people who are called by My name will humble themselves, and pray and seek My face, and turn from their wicked ways, then I will hear from heaven, and will forgive their sin and heal their land.

There is an "if" in this one...a condition. To make an impact on the world, we must first be willing to change ourselves.

15) Ezra 3:11

And they sang responsively, praising and giving thanks to the Lord: "For He is good, for His mercy endures forever toward Israel." Then all the people shouted with a great shout, when they praised the Lord, because the foundation of the house of the Lord was laid.

The laying of a strong foundation was cause for rejoicing. A life built on bedrock of faith will succeed and be happy.

16) Nehemiah 8:10

...Do not sorrow, for the joy of the Lord is your strength.

This prophet knew about building in adversity. He also knew about the joy of the Lord, which gave him the strength to prevail in his conquest. You may likewise see that the Lord, Himself, takes joy in giving you strength.

17) Esther 4:14

...you have come to the kingdom for such a time as this?

Do not give up when you are in a tough place. Your destiny just may depend on one victorious accomplishment.

18) Job 42:10

...And the Lord restored Job's losses when he prayed for his friends...

Job prayed for those who did not deserve it. God notices when our prayers reflect His heart.

19) Psalms 118:8

It is better to trust in the Lord than to put confidence in man.

I do not place my trust in medicine. Things like that can fail. This center verse in the Bible is the schematic that helps balance everything else in life.

20) Proverbs 10:22

The blessing of the Lord makes one rich, and He adds no sorrow with it.

Do you ever question if something is of God? The answer is in this verse. Did it turn out to be a blessing, or did it end in bitter sorrow?

21) Ecclesiastes 3:1

To every thing there is a season, a time for every purpose under the heaven.

Timing is everything. Pray for wisdom to discern the seasons. Then you will have better understanding for God's timing.

22) Song of Solomon 2:4

...his banner over me is love...

The Lord loves you and celebrates your attributes beyond the earthly love that Solomon wrote about. This is a metaphor of Christ's love for you.

23) Isaiah 53:5

But he was wounded for our transgressions, He was bruised for our iniquities, the chastisement of our peace was upon him; and with his stripes we are healed.

All the needs of humankind are in the atonement. The price was paid at Calvary for our sins, failures, and the thing we need so much: peace of mind.

24) Jeremiah 30:17

For I will restore health to you and heal you of your wounds, says the Lord...

This promise was mine. I did not know how, when or why, but I knew I could take this truth to the bank. Make it your promise too.

25) Lamentations 3:23

They (his mercies) are new every morning: great is Your faithfulness.

Since we use up a lot of mercy, let's be thankful

that it is never in short supply.

26) Ezekiel 18:4

...the soul that sins shall die.

We desire a soul and a body that are alive in Christ. I believe this refers to both spiritual and physical death.

27) Daniel 11:32

...the people who know their God shall be strong, and carry out great exploits.

Daniel was a victor in the lion's den because he set himself apart from the excesses of the world. He persevered over all obstacles by prayer.

28) Hosea 4:6

My people are destroyed for lack of knowledge...

Knowledge is power. There is no excuse for ignorance. The age old wisdom of the Bible gives you up-to-date ammunition to win over everything and every situation.

29) Joel 2:28

...I will pour out My spirit upon all flesh; your sons and your daughters shall prophesy, your old men shall dream dreams, your young men shall see visions.

No matter the situation, I invite you to claim this prophecy for yourself and your posterity. "All of our family belong to God and are filled with His spirit." By faith, declare that you are a mover and shaker in the Kingdom of Righteousness.

30) Amos 3:3

Can two walk together, unless they are agreed?

Apply this verse when choosing your life's mate, business partners and all relationships. You will be spared much heartache.

31) Obadiah 3

The pride of your heart has deceived you...

A proud heart lies and distorts judgment. It is the root of relational problems and will cause dysfunction at every level. A humble heart is teachable and open for correction.

32) Jonah 2:7

When my soul fainted within me I remembered the Lord; and my prayer went up to You in Your holy temple.

Jonah's mud involved a whale. A big dose of whale jolts the memory and invokes earnest prayer. God, help us avoid the whale of disobedience.

33) Micah 7:18

...He (God) does not retain His anger forever, because he delights in mercy.

How thankful we ought to be for the gentle mercies of the Lord. We often look at our own failures with a magnifying glass, while He sees us through the blood of the covenant.

34) Nahum 1:7

The Lord is good, a strong hold in the day of trouble; and He knows those who trust in Him.

Bad things happen. More than anything, God desires that we trust Him. Many people place blame on Him when bad things happen. Trouble is the result of Adam and Eve's failure. God abides *through* the trouble.

35) Habakkuk 2:4

...the just shall live by his faith.

Our hearts cannot forget the times we've been in hopeless situations. Jehovah-Jirah shows Himself strong and makes a way in our wilderness places. This world is so volatile. The happy soul depends upon God, not the system.

36) Zephaniah 3:17

The Lord your God in your midst, the Mighty One, will save; He will rejoice over you with gladness, He will quiet you with His love, He will rejoice over you with singing.

God is in the midst of all our strife. Think of His rejoicing over you and singing because of you. It doesn't get better than that!

37) Haggai 2:9

The glory of this latter temple shall be greater than the former, says the Lord of hosts. And in this place I will give peace, says the Lord of hosts.

Israel must never forget what God has slated for the future. We are in covenant partnership, and therefore, recipients of all the promises.

38) Zechariah 4:6

...Not by might, nor by power, but by my spirit, says the Lord of hosts.

"I am weak, but He is strong." Let's sing it with the children.

39) Malachi 3:10

Bring all the tithes into the storehouse, that there may be food in My house, and try Me now in this, says the Lord of hosts, If I will not open the windows of heaven and pour out for you such a blessing that there is not room enough to receive it.

This is the key to everything God has planned for us. When His 10% comes off the top, the 90% is blessed and multiplied.

40) Matthew 7:7

Ask, and it will be given to you; seek, and you will find; knock, and it will be opened to you.

The mouth asks. The eyes seek. The body gets in motion and knocks. God responds.

41) Mark 12:30

...you shall love the Lord your God with all your heart, with all your soul, with all your mind, and with all your strength. This is the first commandment.

The first commandment is obviously the most important. When our love for God is first priority, everything else in life falls into perfect order. Problems start with selfishness, which is opposite of love for God. Rebellion will end in destruction.

42) Luke 18:27

...The things which are impossible with men are possible with God.

Cancer is no bigger challenge for God than a hangnail. Things begin to change when we truly believe that He is able.

43) John 14:27

Peace I leave with you, My peace I give to you; not as the world gives do I give to you. Let not your heart be troubled, neither let it be afraid.

Quote this every day. Jesus gave a command, not

a suggestion. Worry and fear are byproducts of unbelief.

44) Acts 20:35

...It is more blessed to give than to receive.

When a need arises, dig a little deeper and sow a sacrificial seed. The harvest is sure to follow.

45) Romans 8:31

...If God is for us, who can be against us?

The key is being certain that we are *with* God. When our lives align with His Word, we are on the winning team. No weapon can possibly take us down.

46) I Corinthians 2:9

...Eye has not seen, nor ear heard, nor have entered into the heart of man the things which God has prepared for those who love Him.

We aren't home yet. Our finite minds cannot imagine what is waiting for the faithful. Loving and serving God will give entrance to His glories.

47) II Corinthians 12:9

...My grace is sufficient for you; for My strength is made perfect in weakness.

God's grace enables us to do what we could never do alone. Inabilities turn into abilities, by His grace.

48) Galatians 2:20

I have been crucified with Christ; it is no longer I who live, but Christ lives in me; and the life which I now live in the flesh I live by faith in the Son of God, who loved me and gave Himself for me.

I suffered cancer, but I was never alone. When you feel isolated, He is there. He is alive in you and you are reminded, even through your suffering, of His unfailing love.

49) Ephesians 6:12

For we do not wrestle against flesh and blood, but against principalities, against powers, against the rulers of the darkness of this age, against spiritual hosts of wickedness in the heavenly places.

When we fight people, we miss the mark. Spiritual warfare is fought and won on our knees.

50) Philippians 4:13

I can do all things through Christ who strengthens me.

There is no glass ceiling...no limit to the heights we can attain. We must depend upon His strength. We can do exploits through Christ.

51) Colossians 3:2

Set your mind on things above, not on things on this earth.

Materialism is a trap in our affluent society. May God help us balance priorities in these last days.

52) I Thessalonians 5:11

...comfort each other and edify one another...

I would not have made it without the love and support of others. Find someone to encourage today and be God's hand extended.

53) II Thessalonians 2:15

Therefore, brethren, stand fast, and hold the traditions which you were taught...

Godly traditions are sacred. Man's traditions are sometimes empty habits. The key is to discern the difference.

54) I Timothy 6:10

For the love of money is a root of all kinds of evil...

Money is a necessity. The love of money is idolatry, which is the root of every evil on earth.

55) II Timothy 1:7

For God has not given us the spirit of fear; but of power, and of love, and of a sound mind.

Fear is a spirit. We have the authority to rebuke spirits in the name of Jesus.

56) Titus 2:13

...looking for that blessed hope and glorious appearing of our great God and Savior Jesus Christ.

Anticipation of Christ's return puts everything in the right order. When our eyes are set on the blessed hope of His coming, the cares of life do not overwhelm us.

57) Philemon 4

I thank my God, making mention of you always in my prayers...

Deliberately develop the habit of interceding for loved ones in prayer. It is an even greater privilege to pray for those whom you will never see on this earth.

58) Hebrews 11:1

Now faith is the substance of things hoped for, the evidence of things not seen.

Faith is bringing an umbrella when there is not a single cloud in sight.

59) James 5:14

Is anyone among you sick? Let him call for the elders of the church, and let them pray over him, anointing him with oil in the name of the Lord.

The oil is not magic. It is the evidence of faith.

60) I Peter 2:9

But you are a chosen generation, a royal priesthood, a holy nation, His own special people, that you may proclaim the praises of Him who called you out of darkness into His marvelous light.

We were created to praise God and walk in truth. The world is crying for answers. It is our high calling to shine the light of love, so that truth will be seen.

61) II Peter 3:9

The Lord is not slack concerning his promise...

We are human and, too many times, we may doubt. Thankfully, our weaknesses do not negate the promises of God.

62) I John 4:4

...He, who is in you, is greater than he who is in the world.

An army of trouble may surround you. Remember, the enemy is no match for God.

63) II John 6

This is love, that we walk according to His commandments...

The commandments are not friendly tips. They are prerogatives. They were divinely inspired by God for our happiness and good.

64) III John 2

Beloved, I pray that you may prosper in all things and be in health, just as your soul prospers.

God wants us healthy, wealthy and wise.

65) Jude 25

To God our Savior, who alone is wise, be glory and majesty, dominion and power, both now and forever. Amen.

Let our hearts bow in the presence of His Holiness.

66) Revelation 21:4

And God will wipe away every tear from their eyes; there shall be no more death, nor sorrow, nor crying. There shall be no more pain, for the former things have passed away.

With great anticipation, look to the moment when all sorrows of earth will be forever gone. Dark nights of the soul will be no more. These present trials point us to that glorious moment of sweet release when we shall ever be with the Lord.

Acknowledgments

*J*t is my joy to express thanks for those who have helped put this book in your hands.

Vada Allen constantly reminded me that I needed to write this story. Her email notes and our numerous conversations nudged me along. Levoy and I are privileged to attend Oak Hill Assembly of God in Brentwood where her husband, Steve Allen, serves as pastor. Their friendship and encouragement over the years have been priceless.

Pastors Leland and Glenda Hall in Grand Prairie, Texas, opened the doors of their church for our ministry many times. It was there we met Evangelist Daniel Plowman. He spoke a timely word into my life that I should pursue writing (He knew nothing about my aspirations at the time). I knew then it was time to get started.

Jerry and Lucrecia Hobbs are longtime friends. Jerry challenged Levoy and me to escalate the efforts of our ministry to touch more hurting people in these last days. He emphasized that a great part of our endeavors must include authoring books.

My sister-in-law, Sheryl Dewey, dove into the task of editing with her whole heart. Her recall of details and insight was so very helpful. Brother Tim and the congregation of Evangel Temple in San Angelo, Texas, made this book a matter of prayer for many months.

The wise counsel of author, Jason Frenn, showed me the importance of concept and the necessity of proper presentation. His honest evaluation and feedback was monumental in assisting me with the final outcome.

At a time when progress was at a standstill, I felt the need for the input of Jan Larson, my faithful friend and my son-in-law's mother. She was astute in reorganizing my information. I credit her skills in showing me better layout of the text.

Our very dear pastor friends and members of our ministry board, Pastor Bob and Esther Fort, have encouraged me to step out of my comfort zone. We ministered at their churches more than 20 times over the years. Their gentle coaxing has given me the courage to share my heart in speaking, and in the writing of songs and books.

MIRACLE Out of the MUD was birthed after long months of gestation. When the labor pains started, but nothing was moving, I called upon my dear friend, Dr. Peggy Stenger, a pediatric endocrinologist at Children's Hospital in Cincinnati, Ohio. I asked her to edit the medical statements I had written, but Peggy didn't want to assert her opinion and somehow alter the contents. I explained it this way: "When you deliver a baby you help the mother. You don't conceive the child or carry it, but you assist the birthing process. I need your help to birth my 'book baby.'" She was amused by the analogy, empathized with my need, donned the virtual mask and rubber gloves, and went to work.

Friends at Christian Television Networks, including Bob D'Andrea of CTN in Florida, Jerry Rose in Chicago, Garth Coonce with Tri-State Television, and others responded with contributions to help us go to Mexico. Many churches and pastors, the Gospel Music Trust Fund, Dr. Peggy Stenger, John McLaughlin, and a host of caring individuals were among those who sent tangible gifts.

Key people from our church, who have prayed for the completion of this book, have been boosters of my faith. Jane Gibson, Ann Pinder, Ray and Lynn Elder are among those who have expressed their caring and charted its progress.

Our supporters have been essential to birth this project. I deeply appreciate Jerry and Sylvia Hayes for their support, prayers and words of encouragement. Wes Towne, the late Dwight Palser, and Dewayne and Marilyn Bogenhagen have faithfully supported and aligned themselves with the ministry to which we are called.

Dr. Tom and Barbara Taylor came into our lives in God's perfect order. As authors and publishers, they were prepared to make way for a very different miracle. Their calm direction and demeanor during the process has been priceless. Much credit goes to their spiritual discernment and commitment to keep the story authentic.

This book would not be in your hands without the patience of my family. Levoy, Cindy, Suzanne, Mom Dewey and all the family have encouraged me by their enthusiasm. They have been alongside me every step of the way. I love them so very much. We are all Overcomers!

My heartfelt gratitude goes out to countless others and those yet to participate in publishing this personal testimony and instruction. My prayer is that God rewards everyone who has cheered me on, read and helped edit countless pages.

Above all, I thank God for graciously entrusting me with special scars that remind me daily of His mercy and grace. He is the Rock on which I stand.

What others are saying about
MIRACLE *Out of the* MUD

I have read countless books on cancer, most of them very technical. **MIRACLE Out of the MUD***, though it is not medical, is one of the best oncology books out there, for the simple reason that it is not based on theory; it is true life. Cleon Dewey is very transparent as she shares her personal journey of faith to overcome such a tough opponent: cancer. I believe it will be of great encouragement to you."*

Fancisco Contreras, MD
Surgical Oncologist, Oasis of Hope Hospital

A must read! **MIRACLE Out of the MUD** *strikes a deep chord in my spirit. As a missionary/ evangelist, I identify with Cleon's desire to see God's healing come. The Lord has uniquely gifted her and Levoy to take the gospel across this land and around the world. As an author, I have kinship with her desire to propel this triumphant story of surviving two cancers. I continue to be amazed how God has raised her high above this life-threatening storm to touch the souls of hurting people. The value of her journey will instill hope within all who read it.*

Jason Frenn
Missionary/Evangelist

Whenever the Deweys come through the door, I think to myself, "They have it all together." They are committed, beautiful and sweet people. I recommend **MIRACLE Out of the MUD**, *because I know many are walking through the "mud" of life. It is thought provoking and victorious.*

Bob D'Andrea, President and Founder
Christian Television Network

If you are looking for a miracle, read this book! I love the way Cleon's story unfolds. I admire and respect her faith in God, as well as her love of life. I am sure she will touch your heart, as she has touched mine.

Duane Allen, Lead Singer and President
Oak Ridge Boys, Inc.

In her book, **MIRACLE Out of the MUD**, *Cleon Dewey takes us on a "mud journey." God used her to expand on the muddy things in our own lives. She demonstrates how God utilizes these things to get us to the "Water of Life." It is absolutely inspiring! She makes it crystal clear that no matter how muddy things get, God can clean it up and clear it out. This woman is truly the "miracle out of the mud"...you're next!*

Judy Jacobs Tuttle
His Song Ministries
International Institute of Mentoring
Psalmist, Teacher, Author, Humanitarian

Cleon Dewey is a special person. I can take little credit for her remarkable recovery. She brings a smile to my face and inspires others who struggle with hardship and fierce odds.

David R. Spigel, MD
Program Director
Sarah Cannon Cancer Research Center
Nashville, Tennessee

As a physician, I am amazed at the victorious, almost impossible, outcome of Cleon Dewey's battle with cancer. What should have been a terminal illness can be described as no less than a "medical miracle." As her friend, I am in no way surprised. She has the most positive, upbeat attitude of anyone I have ever known. Cleon is at the same time witty and profoundly deep. Her story is one of amazing bravery and courage against incredible odds. So adeptly penned were her words, that I walked where she walked, saw what she saw, and felt what she felt. Her courage, determination and faith turned a desperate situation into victory. This book is, not only an inspiration, but it's a reminder of the importance of faith in the ultimate healing of the human body.

Peggy J. Stenger, D.O., C.C.D.
Assistant Professor of Pediatrics
Cincinnati Children's Hospital

Life would be wonderful if there were never any pain, disappointment or sorrow. When trouble comes, and it will, the way we react is critical. We can either focus on the problems or on God's promises. We know we need to be faith-filled and full of hope, but it is not easy. Cleon Dewey has the credibility to tell us how to look for the blessing instead of breaking under the burden.

MIRACLE Out of the MUD is a great testimony to God's power to heal. It is more...Cleon Dewey teaches us how to take life's difficult challenges and grow during the process. If the needle of your "hope tank" is approaching "Empty," this book is a must read for you.

Alton Garrison
Assistant General Superintendent
Executive Director of Church Ministries and Discipleship
Assemblies of God

I just finished reading Cleon Dewey's moving account of her formidable challenges with cancer. Each page draws the reader closer to the final, inescapable persuasion that Almighty God is intimately and intricately involved in the day-to-day life of every true believer. Filled with humor and warm anecdotal memories, MIRACLE Out of the MUD deals with life "in the trenches." No candy coating in this book! Cleon speaks with candor and transparency about the ups and downs of real life as lived by a real woman with real faith in a real God. Whether laughing, crying or just relating, you will be moved and motivated, challenged and changed as the message of this book captures your heart again and again.

Rev. Robert B. Fort
Chairman, United Evangelical Churches

"In our 35-year friendship with Cleon and Levoy Dewey, we have seen Cleon through several health issues – all challenging – but nothing like her experience with cancer. Her perseverance and "feisty" character has had a permanent impact on us. We are amazed at how she has always depended on the Lord for healing and good health. She is not a cancer survivor; she is a cancer OVERCOMER (Rev. 12:11)! Her testimony is one of hope; it gives reason to fight and to never give up on what God can do. Cleon didn't and she's here to write about it today. **MIRACLE Out of the MUD** *will change the life of one who reads it.*

Pastor Steve Allen
Oak Hill Assembly
Nashville, TN 37220

Your story could be included
in the upcoming book,

Mud Baby Stories.

Find out more. Write to us at...
info@MiracleoutoftheMud.com

www.MiracleoutoftheMud.com

Made in the USA
San Bernardino, CA
16 July 2014